Autism:
A Spiritual Perspective

Practical Tools, Insights, and Exercises for a Fulfilling and Empowered Life for Parents, Professionals, and Advocates

Rev. ORESTE J. DAVERSA

Interfaith Minister

PUBLISHER'S NOTE

This book is designed to provide accurate and authoritative information. information in regard to the subject matter covered. It is sold with the understanding that neither the author nor publisher is engaged in rendering psychological, legal, or other professional service. If psychological, legal, professional advice or other expert assistance is required, the services of a professional in that field should be sought. The principles and concepts presented in this book are the opinions of the author and are based on his interpretations of the aforementioned principles. Neither the author nor publisher is liable or responsible to any person or entity for any errors contained on this book, or website, or for any special, incidental, or consequential damage caused or alleged to be caused directly or indirectly by the information contained on this book or website. Any application of the techniques, ideas, and suggestions in this book is at the reader's sole discretion and risk.

No part of this publication may be reproduced, redistributed, taught, stored in a retrieval system, or transmitted, in any form, or by any means, electronic, mechanical, photocopy, recording, or otherwise, without the prior written permission of the publisher.

Disclosure Statement: This book contains both AI-assisted and AI-generated content. The AI-assisted content was developed using tools to aid in brainstorming, editing, and refining the text, while the AI-generated content includes sections of the book created entirely by artificial intelligence. All AI-generated content has been reviewed and edited to ensure it meets the high standards of quality and originality.

FIRST EDITION

ISBN: 978-1-952294-43-3

Library of Congress Control Number: 2025915166

Published by: Cutting Edge Technology Publishing

Copyright © Oreste J. D'Aversa, 2025. All rights reserved.

TABLE OF CONTENTS

Dedication	7
Disclaimer	9
Preface	11
About the Author	13
Introduction	17
SECTION ONE: For Parents of Autistic Individuals	19
Chapter 1: Seeing the Divine in Your Child	21
Chapter 2: Parenting with Presence	27
Chapter 3: Spiritual Approaches to Sensory Sensitivities	31
Chapter 4: Trusting Their Path	35
Chapter 5: Creating a Sacred Home Environment	41
Chapter 6: Heart-to-Heart Communication	47
Chapter 7: Faith, Hope, and Emotional Strength	53
Chapter 8: Navigating the System with Grace	59
Chapter 9: Celebrating Progress with Gratitude	65
Chapter 10: Siblings and Soul Lessons	71
Chapter 11: Planning with Peace of Mind	77
Chapter 12: You Were Chosen for This Journey	83
SECTION TWO: For Support Professionals	89
Chapter 13: Seeing the Individual Beyond the Label	91

Chapter 14: Creating Sensory and Spirit-Friendly Spaces   97

Chapter 15: Holistic Communication Tools   103

Chapter 16: Being Trauma-Informed and Spiritually-Aware   109

Chapter 17: Recognizing Spiritual Intelligence   115

Chapter 18: Serving the Family as a Whole   121

Chapter 19: Guiding with Meaning and Purpose   127

Chapter 20: Sacred Structure and Routines   133

Chapter 21: Mindfulness and Grounding Practices   139

Chapter 22: Developing Sacred Rapport   145

Chapter 23: Ethical Empowerment   151

Chapter 24: Caring for the Whole Being   157

SECTION THREE: For Autism Advocates   165

Chapter 25: The Spiritual Power of Neurodiversity   167

Chapter 26: Centering Autistic Voices   173

Chapter 27: Dignity for All   183

Chapter 28: Creating Sacred Inclusion   187

Chapter 29: Educating with Love and Light   195

Chapter 30: Language That Honors the Soul   203

Chapter 31: Justice as a Spiritual Imperative   209

Chapter 32: Infusing Policy with Purpose   217

Chapter 33: Empowering the Spirit of the Advocate   225

Chapter 34: Redefining Safety with Compassion	231
Chapter 35: Building Conscious Communities	239
Chapter 36: Affirming Sacred Purpose	247
Conclusion	255
Footnotes	259
Bibliography	267
Glossary of Terms	275
Suggested Reading List	307

THIS PAGE INTENTIONALLY LEFT BLANK

Dedication

To every **Autistic Person** –

You are not a puzzle to be solved, but a soul to be celebrated.

Your presence brings wisdom, depth, and

divine beauty into the world.

To the **Parents** –

Who show up every day with courage, grace, and unconditional

love – your hearts are sacred ground.

To the **Support Professionals** –

Who listen deeply, adapt thoughtfully, and serve with

humility – your care is a quiet revolution.

To the **Advocates** –

Who fight with love, speak with clarity, and carry

hope for all – this book walks beside you in your mission.

THIS PAGE INTENTIONALLY LEFT BLANK

Legal Disclaimer and Author's Intent

This book is a work of spiritual insight, intuitive guidance, and heartfelt compassion created with the sincere desire to support individuals, families, educators, and advocates connected to the autism community. The content is offered not as medical, psychological, or therapeutic advice, but as **a soul-centered contribution rooted in empathy, reverence, and love**.

The author is **not a licensed healthcare provider, psychologist, therapist, or certified autism specialist**. Nothing in this book should be interpreted as a substitute for professional diagnosis, medical treatment, therapeutic intervention, or educational services. **Readers are encouraged to seek the guidance of qualified professionals for any clinical, emotional, or developmental concerns.**

The practices, tools, terms, and spiritual reflections shared in this book are based on **personal study, spiritual observation, intuitive understanding, and experiences as a human being dedicated to compassionate service**. While these ideas are presented in good faith to uplift and inspire, the author makes **no guarantees regarding their applicability or effectiveness** in every situation and disclaims liability for any actions taken based on this material.

At the time of writing and printing, the ideas and information presented herein are either **original contributions** or are based on **freely accessible resources available to the public via the internet**. This book makes no use of proprietary research or copyrighted material without permission.

This book was written **not for fame or prestige, but out of a genuine calling to serve**. It is the author's deepest hope that this work will contribute to a world where individuals on the autism spectrum are **honored, understood, and supported with dignity**. Every page reflects a belief in the sacred worth of every human soul, regardless of neurodiversity.

In sharing this book, the author stands not as an expert, but as a **witness, advocate, and ally** – offering insights intended to encourage **growth, inclusion, love, and understanding** in homes, schools, and communities everywhere.

Preface

A Heartfelt Message from the Author

Dear Reader,

This book was not written from a clinical desk or with academic credentials behind my name – it was born in the quiet spaces of prayer, reflection, and an unshakable calling to serve. It came through whispers of the Spirit, gentle nudges from something higher, and the deep yearning of my own soul to make a difference in a world that often misunderstands or overlooks the sacredness of neurodiversity.

I have never walked in the exact footsteps of an autistic individual. I have not parented a neurodivergent child. I do not hold degrees in psychology or behavioral science. And yet, in my own spiritual journey, I have been led to witness the beauty, the brilliance, and the sacred presence that lives in every person – particularly those whose ways of communicating, connecting, or experiencing the world don't conform to society's expectations.

This book is a response to that calling – a humble offering of words and wisdom that aims to uplift the hearts of autistic individuals, to lighten the burdens of caregivers, and to encourage the many professionals who walk alongside them with devotion and care.

It is not here to fix or pathologize. It is here to *honor, to listen, to hold space,* and to remind all of us that the soul knows no diagnosis.

In these pages, you will not find formulas or prescriptions. You will find spiritual tools, reflective practices, and compassionate perspectives meant to help reframe the autism experience through a sacred lens. You will find language that respects the dignity of each being. You will find pathways that promote emotional safety, soul expression, and inclusive belonging. Most of all, I hope you will find comfort in knowing that you are not alone.

Whether you are a parent waking up in the middle of the night worrying about your child's future, a teacher searching for deeper connection in the classroom, or an autistic adult looking for words that speak to your own sacred worth – may this book be a companion to you.

May it remind you that spirituality is not something separate from neurodiversity – but something that lives *within it*.

With reverence for your journey and hope for our collective healing,

Rev. Oreste J. DAversa,
Author and Advocate for Sacred Inclusion

About the Author

Reverend Oreste J. D'Aversa (O-res-tee DA-versa) is an Interfaith (All-Faiths) Minister ordained by The New Seminary in New York City. Also known as *"Reverend Rusty",* he was raised Catholic and has received the Sacraments of Baptism, Holy Communion, and Confirmation.

He follows the teachings of Jesus the Christ, all of the Prophets, the Ascended Masters, and all those who are and serve the light. He is here to serve GOD and humankind. He is also a Spiritual Guide and Teacher and helps people find their true life's work and their spiritual path.

You can learn more about his work as an Interfaith Minister at **www.GODLovesYouAndMe.org**

He is also the owner of Greater Philadelphia Small Business Services LLC **(PhillyBusinessServices.com)** as a Small Business Coach, Consultant, Trainer, Author, Speaker, Seminar Leader, Public Speaking Coach, and University Lecturer.

He appears as a guest speaker on podcasts, radio, and television discussing his expertise on business-related and personal growth subjects, and has authored numerous books, manuals, articles, and audio CDs.

Books by Rev. Oreste J. DAversa
(Available on Amazon.com):

- I'm a Catholic in the Modern World, What Do I Do After My Confirmation?
- UNPLUGGED! A Practical Guide to Managing Teenage Stress in the Digital Age
- Hey World! Why do I Feel All Alone in a Planet Full of People?
- I Didn't Get a Chance to Say Good-bye ... Now What Can I Do?
- Write Your Own Funeral Service
- Life Beyond the Pandemic: A Practical New Journey Handbook
- Healing the Holes in My Soul!: How I Saved My Own Life, Became Whole to Lead a Happy, Fulfilling and Joyous Life!
- Baby Boomer Entrepreneur: Implementing the Boomer Business Success System The Complete and Proven Guide to Starting a Successful Business, having ... Want while Making a Difference in the World!
- Selling for Non-Selling Professionals©: Learn Basic, Proven and Results Oriented Sales Skills, Methods and Techniques to Get Clients Consistently with No Prior Sales Background and Increase Revenue
- The Resume and Cover Letter Writing Toolkit for the Successful Job Seeker

- **Books by Rev. Oreste J. DAversa (Available on Amazon.com):**

- *Power Interviewing: Proven Job Interview Techniques That Get You Results!*
- *The Step-by-Step Business Networking Kit: The Ultimate Business Networking System that Delivers Superior Results!*
- *SELL More Technology NOW! Proven Sales Methods and Established Practices that Deliver Results*
- *The Seven Simple Principles of Prosperity: Practical Exercises to Achieve a Rich, Happy and Joyous Life!*

THIS PAGE INTENTIONALLY LEFT BLANK

Introduction: A New Way of Seeing

Autism is often introduced to us as a medical diagnosis – defined by criteria, explained in clinical terms, and followed by a list of interventions or therapies. But what if autism is also something more? What if it is not just a neurological difference, but a spiritual calling – an invitation to see the world, ourselves, and one another through a deeper, more compassionate lens?

This book was born out of that question.

As parents, professionals, and advocates, many of us have been taught to focus on "fixing" or "improving" autistic individuals, often with good intentions. But somewhere along the way, something gets lost – the wholeness, the divinity, the radiant uniqueness that each person brings simply by being alive.

Autism: A Spiritual Perspective is a call to return to the sacred. It is a reminder that autistic individuals are not here to conform to our world – they are here to help transform it. Their way of being may challenge the status quo, but it also offers an invitation to slow down, pay attention, and expand our definition of what it means to be human.

This book is divided into three sections: each tailored to a different group of readers:

- For **Parents**, the journey focuses on love, trust, and spiritual growth within the family.

- For **Support Professionals**, it explores soul-centered service, compassionate practice, and whole-person care.

- For **Advocates**, it offers a vision of justice, inclusion, and human dignity rooted in spiritual awareness.

No matter which path brought you to this book, you belong here. You are part of a larger story – one that transcends diagnostic labels and embraces the mystery and magic of neurodiversity. This story is about connection: to ourselves, to others, and to something greater than all of us.

You will find practical tools in these pages – rituals, exercises, communication strategies, and spiritual reflections. But more than that, you will find hope. Hope that our differences do not divide us but deepen us. Hope that every person, regardless of ability, is a vital part of the human family. Hope that we can build a world where every child, teen, and adult on the spectrum is seen, supported, and celebrated for who they truly are.

Let this be your invitation to see autism not just through the lens of science, but through the eyes of the soul. Let it remind you that you are not alone, that healing is possible, and that love is always the most powerful tool we have.

Welcome to the journey.
Let us walk it with reverence.

SECTION ONE:
For Parents of Autistic Individuals

Theme: Love, Trust, Growth, and Sacred Responsibility

Parenting a child on the autism spectrum is a spiritual journey filled with profound love, inner transformation, and deep soul lessons. This section is written to support parents in shifting from fear to faith, confusion to clarity, and exhaustion to empowered presence. Through spiritually grounded insights and practical tools, you'll discover how to create a peaceful home environment, honor your child's divine uniqueness, and grow spiritually as a parent. These chapters will help you embrace your sacred role while nurturing a purposeful, fulfilling, and empowered life for both your child and yourself.

NOTES:

Chapter 1: Seeing the Divine in Your Child

To truly see the divine in your child with autism is to experience parenting not merely as a responsibility but as a sacred spiritual journey. It is a call to rise above social expectations, diagnostic labels, and comparison traps, and instead meet your child with reverence, wonder, and radical love. When viewed through the lens of spirit rather than limitation, autism is not a problem to solve but a form of divine expression to honor. Every child carries a unique soul blueprint, and autism may reflect a heightened sensitivity to truth, energy, and purpose.

As a parent, your sacred role is not to mold your child into someone else's ideal – but to meet them, love them, and grow alongside them in their natural, divinely intended design. That love must begin with a shift in perception. Many parents receive a diagnosis with understandable grief. The imagined future, the dreams that were once held, may dissolve in an instant. But beyond the grief lies a deeper invitation – to awaken. To recognize that your child is not broken but born to be different. And that difference holds purpose. It is not an error, but a sacred variation in the human tapestry.[1]

Spiritual parenting begins not with control, but with curiosity. Ask not, "How do I change my child to fit?" but rather, "What is this child here to teach me?" This single question can transform your home, your mindset, and your heart. Children on the autism spectrum are often attuned to energies and truths that defy words. They may resist societal scripts not because they are defiant, but because they are aligned with a different frequency.

Divine presence can be seen in your child's eyes, heard in their hums and rhythms, and felt in their silence. What the clinical world labels as "stimming" or "restricted behaviors" can also be interpreted, from a spiritual view, as rituals – movements that regulate their energy or communicate truths beyond language.[2] What appears to be disinterest might be energetic self-preservation. What seems like resistance could be a boundary rooted in self-awareness.

Spiritual traditions around the world have long recognized that those who walk differently among us often carry sacred insight. In many indigenous cultures, neurodivergent individuals were seen as medicine carriers, wisdom keepers, or spirit walkers – people born to reveal what others overlook.[3] You do not need to share these cosmologies to acknowledge a core truth: your child has value far beyond what is measurable, and their essence is worth celebrating, not just accommodating.

This sacred lens requires us to slow down. Our culture prizes productivity, timelines, and checklists. But the soul has no use for deadlines. If your child spends thirty minutes twirling with joy, that is not time lost; it is spirit expressed. Sitting in silence, lining up objects, or repeating phrases may not fit the mold of traditional learning, but they may be spiritual acts of organization, grounding, or reverence.[4] We must let go of the impulse to interrupt these moments and instead learn from them.

Emotional and energetic attunement is vital. Your child may not always communicate with words, but they constantly read your energy. When you are anxious, distracted, or impatient, they feel it. Conversely, when you ground yourself in peace through breath, prayer, or meditation, you become a safe energetic field for them.[5] You don't have to be perfect. But you are invited to become intentional.

To be a spiritual parent is not to avoid mistakes, but to learn from them. There will be days of overwhelm, frustration, and fear. You are human, and this path is not linear. What matters most is your willingness to return – to love, to presence, to faith. Extend compassion to yourself as freely as you extend it to your child. This too is part of your sacred practice.

You are not raising a "case" or a "condition." You are raising a soul. One who may see the world differently, move through it differently, and engage it differently – but one who is no less whole. Speak blessings over their life. Honor their inner rhythm. Celebrate their wins, however small they may seem. And in moments of uncertainty, remember: your presence, your stillness, and your love are often more healing than any plan.

This journey will change you. It will stretch you, soften you, and awaken parts of you that you may have forgotten. It may ask you to release the illusion of control, but in return, it offers the gift of surrender. You may grieve the path you thought you'd walk, only to find the one you're walking is more sacred than you ever imagined.

In the end, seeing the divine in your child is not about theology or belief systems. It's about presence. It's about choosing to see the light that lives within them, especially on the days it feels dim. It's about honoring their life as meaningful, their pace as perfect, and their soul as sovereign.

Practical Exercise: Sacred Observation Practice

Choose a 15-minute window during your day when your child is fully engaged in a preferred activity.

1. Sit nearby without engaging, correcting, or redirecting.

2. Observe their body language, energy, rhythm, and emotion.

3. Journal afterward:

   - What did I see that was sacred?

   - What shifted in me as I watched?

   - What did I learn about my child's essence?

Repeat this practice three times this week. Over time, it will deepen your ability to perceive the divine spark in your child and remind you of the sacred connection you both share.

_____

_____

_____

_____

_____

_____

_____

_____

NOTES:

Chapter 2: Parenting with Presence

In a world that moves fast and demands more, parenting with presence can feel like a revolutionary act. Yet for the parent of a child on the autism spectrum, presence is not only a gift – it's a spiritual necessity. Presence is not simply being in the same room. It's the art of being emotionally, mentally, and energetically attuned to your child. It's the sacred pause, the deep breath, the full-body yes to the moment as it is.

Children with autism often resist surface-level interactions. They may not respond to verbal cues or social conventions the way others do. But they are extraordinarily perceptive when it comes to energy, tone, and intention.[1] This means your presence – not your plans, not your perfection – is what your child most needs. When you show up fully, you create a sanctuary where safety, trust, and connection can bloom.

Presence is also a mirror. Children often reflect the inner world of their parents. If you are anxious, rushed, or distracted, they may become agitated or withdrawn.[2] But when you are centered and calm, you offer them a nonverbal invitation into peace. This isn't about being perfect – it's about being real and choosing again and again to return to the moment, especially when it's hard.

Many spiritual traditions teach that presence is the gateway to divine connection. The mystics, sages, and saints across centuries practiced stillness and mindfulness not to escape the world, but to fully meet it.[3] You don't need a mountaintop retreat to be spiritually present. The sacred is available in your kitchen, your car, or the grocery store aisle. Every meltdown, every bedtime, every quiet moment is a potential altar.

Presence is not passive. It is a form of active listening, of energetic participation in your child's experience. When your child flaps their hands, hums repetitively, or spins in circles, your job is not to stop them – it is to observe, to connect, and to understand. These are not distractions from the moment; they _are_ the moment.[4]

Technology and task-driven living often pull us away from this awareness. You may be tempted to scroll, multitask, or emotionally check out – especially during difficult behaviors. But parenting with presence means resisting the urge to flee. It means anchoring your awareness in the now, not in the hypothetical future or the story of what's going wrong. Presence is not about controlling outcomes; it's about transforming how you meet them.

This also includes being present with yourself. Too often, parents give so much that they forget to check in with their own inner needs. Being present means honoring your exhaustion, your fears, your moments of sadness.[5] When you meet yourself without judgment, you model for your child how to do the same.

Some days, presence means deep listening. Other days, it means silence. Sometimes it means offering space. Other times, it means sitting close. There is no formula. Presence is less about what you do and more about who you are in the doing. When your child senses that you are truly with them—not trying to fix or rush or distract – they begin to trust you with their inner world.

You are not required to know all the answers. What is asked of you is your presence. In moments of chaos, take a breath. In moments of confusion, soften your body. In moments of despair, place your hand on your heart. These small acts of presence accumulate into an atmosphere of sacred safety.

In the long run, your presence will be remembered more than your solutions. Your stillness will echo louder than your corrections. Your compassion will outlast your strategies. Presence is not the tool you use – it is the sacred space you *become.*

Practical Exercise: Five-Minute Presence Ritual

Use this exercise once daily to re-center yourself before or during parenting moments.

1. Find a quiet place and sit comfortably.

2. Close your eyes. Inhale deeply for a count of four, hold for four, and exhale for four. Repeat this cycle three times.

3. Place one hand on your chest, the other on your belly. Say silently: "I am here. I am safe. I am enough."

4. Picture your child's face. Send them silent blessings or loving-kindness.

5. Open your eyes and re-enter the moment with intentional awareness.

Repeat as often as needed to return to presence, especially in challenging situations.

_____

_____

_____

_____

_____

_____

_____

Chapter 3: Spiritual Approaches to Sensory Sensitivities

Sensory sensitivities are among the most commonly misunderstood aspects of autism. To many, they appear as overreactions or behavioral problems. But from a spiritual perspective, they are not flaws – they are signals. They reveal a nervous system wired with heightened perception and a soul attuned to subtler frequencies of the world. When we approach sensory sensitivities spiritually, we shift from reacting to behaviors to honoring boundaries.

Children with autism often experience sound, light, texture, or movement more intensely than neurotypical individuals.[1] A flickering light can feel like lightning. A scratchy tag may feel like burning fabric. A loud cafeteria can be disorienting. These are not signs of weakness but indicators of profound sensory sensitivity. Spiritually, this sensitivity can be seen as a gift – an ability to perceive nuances others overlook.

In spiritual traditions, sensitivity is often associated with higher levels of awareness.[2] Mystics, empaths, and prophets have long been described as people who feel deeply, sense beyond the physical, and intuit energies others ignore. Your child may be such a soul – sensitive not just in body but also in spirit. They may read your mood before you speak or react strongly to environments charged with stress, even if no words are exchanged.

Instead of trying to toughen them up or force them to adjust, spiritual parenting invites you to co-create sensory safety. This means becoming attuned to your child's preferences and designing routines, spaces, and relationships that support their nervous system. It means recognizing that meltdowns are not tantrums – they are the body's alarm system saying, "I'm overwhelmed."[3]

Begin by observing how your child reacts to various sensory inputs: lighting, sound levels, clothing, smells, textures, and food. These reactions are sacred clues. Keeping a sensory journal can help identify triggers and preferences. This is not just data collection – it's soul listening. It shows your child that their experiences matter and that their body is wise.

Spiritually safe spaces are environments where your child feels energetically and physically supported. This might mean dimming the lights, turning off background music, or using noise-canceling headphones. It might include sensory-friendly textures like soft fabrics, weighted blankets, or fidget tools. Each adaptation is not an indulgence – it is an act of reverence.

Grounding practices can also help regulate sensory input. Deep pressure hugs, rhythmic breathing, movement rituals, or spending time in nature are powerful tools.[4] Encourage your child to develop their own calming rituals. Some may find peace in repetitive movements, drawing mandalas, or listening to calming frequencies. Let these practices be framed as sacred – not strange. The soul knows how to self-heal when given permission.

When sensory overload happens, your presence is the most powerful medicine. Sit near without judgment. Offer silence over solutions. Let your calm nervous system become the anchor. This moment isn't about correcting – it's about co-regulating. Your grounded energy sends the message: "You're safe. I'm here. We will move through this together."[5]

Sensory experiences also hold spiritual meaning. What your child finds soothing or distressing may carry symbolic significance. A child drawn to water may be intuitively cleansing their energy. One who avoids crowds may be protecting their aura. Explore these connections with curiosity and respect. You're not diagnosing – you're discovering.

In time, you may find that your child's sensitivities are not barriers to be removed but portals to deeper understanding. They teach you to slow down, to listen more deeply, to notice the world with reverence. In this way, spiritual parenting is not just about helping your child – it's about being transformed by them.

Practical Exercise: Creating a Sacred Sensory Space

Choose a space in your home to transform into a sensory sanctuary for your child.

1. Ask yourself: What calms or soothes my child? What triggers them?

2. Use their input (verbal or behavioral) to choose elements:
   - Lighting (dim, natural, colored lamps?)
   - Sound (quiet, music, white noise?)
   - Texture (pillows, rugs, blankets, bean bags?)
   - Smell (essential oils, or none at all?)

3. Add 1 spiritual element (e.g., calming affirmation, symbol, or object that offers peace).

4. Let your child help set it up and personalize it.

5. Visit this space daily – even for a few minutes – to reinforce that peace is always accessible.

_____

_____

_____

_____

_____

Chapter 4: Trusting Their Path

One of the greatest spiritual challenges in parenting a child with autism is surrendering the illusion of control. As parents, we want to guide, plan, and protect. We crave reassurance that everything will turn out well. Yet spiritual parenting invites us into a different posture – not one of control, but of **trust**. Not trust in outcomes, but trust in *the path itself*.

Trusting your child's path means honoring that their journey may not follow conventional timelines or milestones. It means letting go of comparisons, diagnosis-based projections, and societal standards. It means believing, even when you don't fully understand, that your child is unfolding exactly as they are meant to – and that you are, too.[1]

The need to "fix" or "correct" often arises from fear. Fear that your child won't be accepted. Fear that their life won't be successful or fulfilling. But what if success is not measured by grades, jobs, or accolades, but by authenticity, peace, and spiritual alignment? What if your child's nontraditional path holds sacred wisdom not just for them, but for you?

Children on the spectrum often take nonlinear routes. Progress may come in waves. Skills may emerge and recede. One day may be full of joyful breakthroughs, the next filled with frustration.

Trusting their path means seeing this not as regression or failure, but as part of a deeper rhythm.[2] Nature doesn't grow in straight lines – neither do souls.

There will be moments when professionals, educators, or even well-meaning friends imply that your child is falling behind. In those moments, remember: the only path your child needs to be on is *their own*. Your sacred task is not to push them faster, but to walk beside them, celebrating their steps, however small or slow.

In spiritual terms, every soul comes into this life with a unique curriculum.[3] Your child's sensitivities, preferences, gifts, and challenges are all part of a greater unfolding. You are not the author of their destiny – you are a loving witness to it. And sometimes, trusting their path means releasing your own need for certainty.

This trust also requires discernment. It doesn't mean becoming passive or giving up on interventions. It means choosing support that align with your child's spirit, not just their symptoms. It means asking not only "What will help them succeed?" but also "What honors their essence?"

Daily spiritual practices can help you cultivate this trust. Prayer, meditation, journaling, or silent reflection ground you in the truth that your child's journey is not random. It is purposeful. It is sacred. When doubts arise – as they will – return to stillness and ask: "What if everything is unfolding perfectly, even if I can't yet see the why?"

Your child may not always meet external expectations, but they will meet divine purpose.[4] A child who doesn't speak may communicate through art or energy. A teen who resists routines may be learning deep spiritual autonomy. A young adult who struggles with employment may be modeling a different kind of meaningful life.

Trusting their path also means trusting yourself. You were chosen as their parent for a reason. You have the instincts, strength, and wisdom required. You may not feel ready – but readiness is often revealed in the walking. You don't have to know the whole path to take the next step.

Let go of the need to rush. Let go of timelines. Let go of fixing. Stand as a guardian of their light, not a mechanic of their behaviors. Be the one who believes in their soul's journey when others focus only on performance. Your faith in them will become a compass they carry forever.

In the end, trusting their path is not just a gift to your child – it is a gift to yourself. It frees you from the burden of control. It opens you to wonder, patience, and peace. And it aligns your parenting with something greater than plans: the mystery and majesty of love unfolding.

Practical Exercise: The Sacred Timeline Journal

Once a week, take 10 – 15 minutes to journal responses to the following prompts:

1. What external expectations have I felt pressured by this week?

2. What evidence have I seen of my child's unique rhythm or gifts?

3. Where can I release control and trust more deeply in their process?

4. What step can I take to honor *their* path – not the world's version of it?

Over time, this practice will train your mind and spirit to embrace your child's journey with more peace and presence.

_____
_____
_____
_____
_____
_____
_____
_____

NOTES:

Chapter 5: Creating s Sacred Home Environment

Home is the first spiritual classroom for a child with autism. It is more than shelter – it is sanctuary. The energy, structure, and intentionality you bring into the home can either soothe or stimulate, ground or overwhelm. Creating a sacred home environment isn't about perfection – it's about presence, rhythm, and reverence for your child's unique spiritual and sensory needs.

For a child on the autism spectrum, the home can feel either like a refuge or a battleground. Many children with autism are acutely sensitive to sound, light, touch, scent, and even the emotional states of others.[1] A sacred home honors these sensitivities not as obstacles to overcome but as wisdom to learn from. When you view the home through the lens of spirit, you begin to see it as a temple – one where healing, connection, and soul growth happen every day.

Begin by creating energetic peace. Your own nervous system sets the tone.[2] Children feel your stress before you speak it. Establishing even a simple practice like beginning your day with a moment of silence, prayer, or breathwork can ripple calm throughout the household. Your child may not articulate it, but they notice when the atmosphere feels safe.

Order and rhythm are also sacred tools. Children with autism often find comfort in predictability.[3] A visual schedule, a familiar order of activities, or even daily rituals (like lighting a candle before dinner or a short blessing before bed) can offer grounding. These aren't just routines – they are spiritual anchors that help your child feel held by something greater than the chaos of the outside world.

Next, consider the sensory field of your home. Reduce clutter, soften lighting, and create quiet zones. Choose natural materials when possible – wood, cotton, plants, and warm, muted colors often feel more soothing than synthetic, overstimulating environments.[4] Have one room or corner dedicated to sensory decompression: a bean bag chair, calming textures, dim light, weighted blankets, or headphones. This is not indulgence – it's sacred design.

Sound matters. Eliminate harsh background noise. Replace television chatter or sudden volume spikes with soft music, nature sounds, or silence.[5] If your child is soothed by repetition or humming, treat it like a spiritual chant, not a nuisance. Learn their sacred sounds and make space for them.

Scents can also be powerful spiritual cues. Light incense, diffuse calming essential oils (like lavender or frankincense), or bake familiar foods that remind them of love and safety. Remember: your child's senses are often pathways to comfort and connection. Scent, sound, and texture are more than inputs – they're invitations to feel at home in the world.

The spiritual atmosphere is just as important. Fill your home with loving speech, respectful language, and affirmations. Let your child hear you speak blessings over them. Let them see you model forgiveness and grace. A sacred home is not free from difficulty – it is filled with practices that return everyone to peace when challenges arise.

Incorporate visual symbols of love, faith, or connection – photos of loved ones, sacred texts, artwork your child has made, or spiritual icons. These are not decorations; they're anchors of belonging. They remind your child that they are safe, seen, and held – by you and by something greater.

Limit digital chaos. Too much screen time can dysregulate your child's nervous system and be distracting from the calming tone you're building. Use technology intentionally: as a learning tool, a sensory break, or connection – not as a default setting for everyday life.[6] Let human presence – not screens – be the center of your home's spiritual energy.

Above all, create a culture of honor. Honor your child's voice, even when it's not verbal. Honor their rhythms, even when they're inconvenient. Honor your own needs, so you don't burn out. A sacred home isn't one where everything is easy – it's one where everything is held in love.

The environment you shape will not only support your child's sensory and emotional well-being – it will shape their sense of spiritual safety in the world. They will carry that safety with them long after they leave your home. It will become their internal sanctuary.

Practical Exercise: Sacred Space Assessment

This week, choose one room or area in your home to spiritually and sensorially transform.

1. Sit quietly in the space for 5 minutes. What do you hear, feel, smell, and sense?

2. Ask these questions:
   - What feels peaceful here?
   - What feels chaotic or overstimulating?
   - What would support more calm and connection?

3. Make 3 small changes – remove a visual distraction, introduce a calming item, or adjust lighting.

4. Invite your child to spend time there. Watch how they respond.

Do this exercise once per week for 4 weeks in different rooms.

Document changes in your child's behavior or energy.

_____

_____

_____

_____

_____

_____

_____

_____

NOTES:

Chapter 6: Heart-to-Heart Communication

Communication is often thought of in terms of spoken language. For parents of autistic individuals, however, communication requires a deeper, more intuitive form of connection. In many cases, the traditional modes of verbal expression may be limited, delayed, or simply different. Yet, beneath the surface lies a vibrant world of connection waiting to be accessed. Heart-to-heart communication is about tuning in – not just with your ears, but with your soul.

At its core, this kind of communication honors the truth that every soul, regardless of verbal ability or cognitive profile, seeks connection. Autistic individuals often express themselves through behavior, energy, and presence. What may seem like silence or withdrawal to the untrained eye can, in fact, be a profound invitation to deeper understanding. The first step for any parent is to quiet their own mental chatter and become an observer – not of symptoms, but of soul cues[1].

Begin by noticing non-verbal signals: facial expressions, body movements, breathing rhythms, and eye contact (or lack thereof). These are all modes of spiritual communication. Many parents describe moments of unspoken knowing – when they simply feel their child's needs, emotions, or intentions.

These experiences are not imaginary; they are the essence of heart-based connection. Trusting these moments strengthens your intuitive muscle and deepens the bond with your child[2].

Practicing heart-to-heart communication starts with presence. Being fully present means putting away distractions, calming your own nervous system, and inviting your child's energy into your awareness. Even sitting silently together can be a sacred act of unity. In those quiet spaces, communication often flows without words. Your calm, loving presence creates an energetic environment where your child feels safe to express themselves[3].

This level of presence also means resisting the urge to rush into solutions. Often, parents feel an internal pressure to "fix" behaviors or quickly resolve emotional outbursts. But what if your child isn't asking for solutions – just understanding? Slowing down and responding with compassion rather than correction can transform the atmosphere between you. Heart-to-heart communication is as much about *receiving* as it is about *giving*. By validating your child's experience, you offer them dignity and safety in simply being who they are.

Intuition plays a vital role here. Many spiritually aware parents report sudden insights or inner promptings about their child's emotional state, preferences, or even spiritual needs. This intuitive sensitivity can be cultivated through prayer, meditation, journaling, and intentional silence. As you develop this capacity, you'll notice fewer misunderstandings and more moments of peaceful resonance[4].

Another essential aspect is energetic empathy – the ability to feel what your child may be experiencing emotionally or energetically. This doesn't mean absorbing their pain but rather being attuned to their frequency. If your child enters a room and you sense tension, anxiety, or joy without a spoken word, that's energetic empathy at work. Responding with love, calm energy, and grounded presence can shift the atmosphere and encourage co-regulation.

Some parents may discover that their children communicate most effectively during motion or activity. Whether it's swinging at the park, pacing through a hallway, or fidgeting with a sensory tool, movement can be a conduit for expression. Pay attention to these moments of motion-based communication. You might find that your child becomes more emotionally available or expressive when their body is allowed to move freely.

Technology can also assist in building heart-to-heart communication. Augmentative and Alternative Communication (AAC) devices, symbol cards, or custom visual boards can bridge gaps between thought and expression. When used with spiritual intention and patience, these tools become vessels for the soul's voice. Celebrate every effort your child makes to connect, whether it's tapping a screen, pointing to a picture, or simply reaching out a hand.

Sacred rituals can also support connection. Try lighting a candle before bedtime, saying a blessing over a meal, or engaging in a daily gratitude practice together. These moments of shared spiritual rhythm establish a pattern of trust and unity. They signal to your child, "We are connected. I see you. I hear you – even without words."

Lastly, remember that your child may be communicating with you on levels you haven't yet recognized. Dreams, synchronicities, shared emotional shifts – all of these can be part of the sacred dialogue between parent and child. Be open to receiving messages in unexpected ways. Keep a journal of your experiences and reflect on how your spiritual bond is evolving.

In a world that often prioritizes verbal fluency, heart-to-heart communication reminds us that the deepest connections transcend words. By slowing down, listening with the soul, and honoring every moment of presence, you enter into a divine relationship that nourishes both you and your child.

Practical Exercise: The Soul Listening Practice

Time Required: 10–15 minutes

1. Find a quiet, comfortable space where you and your child can sit together.

2. Close your eyes for a few moments and take three deep, grounding breaths.

3. Gently place one hand over your heart and the other over your child's (if they allow).

4. Focus your attention on the space between you – not on thoughts or expectations.

5. In silence, simply observe. What do you feel? What emotions arise? Do any images, words, or sensations surface?

6. After a few minutes, gently open your eyes and smile at your child.

7. End the practice by saying aloud or silently, "I am here. I love you. I hear you."

Repeat this practice daily or weekly to strengthen your intuitive bond.

_____

_____

_____

NOTES:

Chapter 7: Faith, Hope, and Emotional Strength

Parenting an autistic child often brings moments of profound love – and profound exhaustion. Between navigating meltdowns, advocating at IEP (Individualized Education Program) meetings, managing therapies, and attending to family life, it can be easy for parents to feel emotionally depleted. Yet amid these challenges, a sacred truth emerges: *you are not alone*. Through the spiritual tools of faith, hope, and daily resilience, parents can find renewal and strength that not only sustains them but uplifts the entire family.

Faith, in this context, isn't limited to religious doctrine. It's the deep spiritual trust that your child's path has meaning. That *your* path, too, has purpose. Faith allows you to believe that even when progress seems slow or uncertainty feels overwhelming, there is a divine order unfolding. This kind of spiritual anchoring does not erase the hard days – it simply helps you walk through them with steadier feet[1].

Hope is the light that keeps you going. Not the kind of hope that denies reality or sugarcoats struggle, but the kind that whispers, *"There is more to this story."* Hope reminds you that your child is growing in unseen ways, that change is always possible, and that love is never wasted. It gives parents' permission to dream, to envision joy, to see beyond diagnoses and into divine possibility[2].

Emotional strength, however, is what ties it all together. It's the ability to return to love again and again – even when your nerves are frayed. It's the daily decision to show up with compassion, to recover after emotional burnout, and to forgive yourself for not being perfect. Emotional strength doesn't mean being unaffected. It means learning to rise after being knocked down[3].

Practically speaking, how can parents build this spiritual-emotional foundation? It begins with rituals of renewal. Whether it's five minutes of deep breathing in the car, a prayer whispered while folding laundry, or journaling at night with a cup of tea, these small spiritual practices have a cumulative effect. They send a signal to your nervous system – and to your soul – that you are supported, guided, and not alone.

Equally powerful is the decision to ground your day with intention. Begin each morning with a brief affirmation or mantra. One mother writes the words "Faith and Flow" on a sticky note each day and places it by her kitchen sink. Another parent starts their day with the question, *"How can I show love today, even in difficulty?"* These sacred cues provide spiritual scaffolding during even the most chaotic days.

It's also important to reframe setbacks. When therapies stall, behaviors escalate, or family dynamics become strained, it's easy to feel like progress has vanished. But the spiritual perspective asks us to look deeper: What are we being invited to learn here? Is this a moment to practice patience, surrender control, or ask for help? Seen through the lens of growth, even the hardest moments hold sacred value[4].

Community is another wellspring of strength. Whether it's a faith group, an online support forum, or a trusted friend who truly listens, being surrounded by others who *see* you is spiritually nourishing. Isolation breeds discouragement, but community breathes life into tired spirits. Don't be afraid to seek out spiritual companionship – it's not a weakness, it's wisdom.

Parents must also give themselves grace. You will lose your temper. You will forget appointments. You will cry in your car. None of this means you are failing – it means you are human. And in your humanity, you are modeling resilience. Every time you apologize, try again, or admit you need rest, you are teaching your child emotional honesty. That is sacred parenting.

Developing emotional strength also includes becoming aware of emotional cycles. Pay attention to the times of day or week when you feel most drained. Are mornings frantic? Do weekends feel lonely? Build gentle rhythms around these emotional valleys. A walk at sunset, a call to a friend, or a no-phone Sunday can help stabilize the emotional terrain.

Never underestimate the healing power of spiritual language. Speaking faith-filled truths aloud – especially in the presence of your child – shifts the energy in your home. Try simple statements like: "You are deeply loved," "We are growing together," or "GOD is with us in this." These affirmations don't just support your child – they replenish you, too.

Lastly, anchor yourself in something larger than the present moment. Whether you believe in GOD, the universe, divine intelligence, or simply the mystery of life – lean into that. Remember, you are part of a sacred ecosystem, where no effort is wasted, and no love is lost. Trust that your path is held by something greater than circumstance.

When faith roots your heart, hope lights your path, and emotional strength carries you forward, you begin to transform not only your parenting – but your entire life. The storms still come, but you become the calm within them. You begin to parent not from depletion, but from devotion. And that changes everything.

Practical Exercise: The Resilience Anchor

Time Required: 10 minutes

1. Find a quiet space and sit comfortably.
2. Take 3 deep breaths, feeling the rise and fall of your body.
3. Place a hand on your heart and close your eyes.
4. Silently repeat the following phrases, or adapt your own:
    - "I am doing my best."
    - "This moment is hard, but it will pass."
    - "Love is guiding me."
5. Think of one way you showed emotional strength in the last week. Recall it vividly.
6. Now, imagine yourself offering that same strength again – calm, grounded, and loving.
7. Open your eyes and give thanks for that strength.

Repeat whenever you feel emotionally worn down.

_____
_____
_____
_____
_____
_____

NOTES:

Chapter 8: Navigating the System with Grace

Navigating the medical, educational, and social systems as a parent of an autistic child can feel like entering a maze without a map. Forms, appointments, evaluations, therapies, funding programs – all vital, yet often overwhelming. And for many parents, the systems themselves can seem cold, bureaucratic, or even dismissive. But what if we could bring *grace* into the process? What if spiritual strength and emotional steadiness could guide us through the red tape and resistance?

To navigate with grace means to move through challenges without losing your center. Grace doesn't imply weakness or passivity – it is active, grounded, and powerful. It's the calm voice in a crowded office. It's the composed tone in a contentious IEP (Individualized Education Program) meeting. It's the steady breath you take before advocating once more for your child's needs.

The first spiritual tool for navigating the system is **clarity**. Clarity is born from quiet. Begin each week, or each new process, with a moment of stillness. Ask yourself: *What is the next right step for my child? What is mine to carry – and what can I release?* When you pause and listen, inner wisdom surfaces. You can then take action from a place of purpose, not panic[1].

The second tool is **intention**. Before making a phone call, attending a meeting, or writing an email, set an internal intention. Say silently or aloud, "May I speak with compassion and clarity. May my words be rooted in love." This intention-setting shifts your energy. You enter difficult systems as a spiritual advocate, not just a stressed-out parent.

Documentation is another sacred practice. Keep a journal or digital folder of every interaction – dates, names, conversations, and outcomes. Not only is this practical, it's spiritually grounding. Writing things down transfers your emotional burden into structured form. You'll be better prepared, and less likely to feel lost in a storm of information.

One of the hardest parts of navigating the system is encountering resistance: denied services, insensitive professionals, or unreturned phone calls. In these moments, the spiritual principle of **non-reactivity** becomes a superpower. Reactivity is natural – but it rarely serves your highest good. Non-reactivity means choosing your response instead of being hijacked by the moment. Take a breath. Count to three. Write the angry email – but don't send it yet. Respond, don't react[2].

At the same time, grace includes **righteous assertiveness**. Your child's needs matter. Your voice carries weight. Speaking with grace doesn't mean staying silent. It means grounding your advocacy in truth and love. Instead of "You never listen to me," try "I'd like to revisit what's best for my child and explore options together." This spiritual diplomacy invites collaboration without compromising strength[3].

Another powerful practice is **visualization**. Before entering any system – a school, a clinic, a government office – pause and visualize the energy you want to bring. Picture yourself calm, wise, and steady. Imagine a sphere of peaceful light around you and your child. You are not walking in alone. You are surrounded by spiritual support, even in secular spaces.

Mantras and affirmations can also provide spiritual armor. Here are a few examples:

- "I am my child's safe place and sacred voice."
- "We are guided. We are protected."
- "Truth, love, and wisdom go before me."

Repeat your mantra before any system-based interaction. Let it recalibrate your nervous system and remind you of your sacred mission.

Finding **allies within the system** is another grace strategy. Not everyone in the system is cold or indifferent. Many educators, caseworkers, and clinicians are deeply compassionate – they're just stretched thin. When you find someone who genuinely cares, nurture that relationship. Express gratitude. Build rapport. Allies help you navigate the maze with more ease and effectiveness.

When burnout hits – and it will – return to **rest and restoration**. Navigating the system is labor-intensive, emotionally draining work. Give yourself spiritual permission to pause. A nap, a walk, a worship service, or five minutes of silence in your car can restore what systems deplete. Self-care isn't selfish – it's strategic.

Discernment is also key. Not every recommendation is right for your child. Just because a professional suggests something doesn't mean it aligns with your child's needs or spirit. Ask, *Does this resonate? Will this empower or diminish my child?* Let your intuition weigh in alongside the data.

It's equally important to understand your **rights and resources**. Grace does not exclude research. In fact, learning your rights is an act of spiritual empowerment. Read books. Join support groups. Know the laws. The more informed you are, the more confidently you can advocate – and the more gracefully you can push back when necessary[4].

Lastly, never forget the power of **spiritual surrender**. There will be delays. Mistakes. Doors that seem closed. In these moments, surrender does not mean giving up – it means giving over. Hand the struggle to GOD, the Universe, or whatever sacred force you trust. Say, "Guide me. Go before me. Make a way where I cannot see one." Surrender creates space for miracles.

Navigating systems is not just a logistical challenge – it's a spiritual path. Each form, meeting, and appointment can be part of your family's sacred unfolding. When you walk this path with clarity, compassion, intention, and grace, you don't just survive the system – you soften it. You infuse it with soul. You become a quiet revolutionary.

And one day, long after the meetings and paperwork are done, your child will know: *My parent walked through the fire – and carried light with them.*

Practical Exercise: The Spiritual Advocacy Plan

Time Required: 15 minutes

1. Choose one system you're currently navigating (e.g., school, healthcare, therapy).

2. Sit quietly and reflect on your current challenges within that system.

3. Write down the following:

   - The main goal you want to achieve.
   - The emotions you're currently carrying.
   - One spiritual intention for your next interaction.
   - One practical step you can take this week.

4. Create a mantra to support you (e.g., "Peace and truth guide my voice").

5. Keep this plan visible as a spiritual anchor.

Repeat as needed for each major system you interact with.

_____

_____

_____

_____

_____

_____

Chapter 9: Celebrating Progress with Gratitude

In a world that often measures success through milestones, grades, and clinical charts, the unique journey of raising an autistic child calls for a different compass – one grounded in **gratitude** and spiritual awareness. Progress for our children is often non-linear, subtle, and deeply personal. A single word spoken after weeks of silence. A moment of eye contact. A day without a meltdown. These are sacred victories. They may not make headlines, but they shift universes.

Celebrating progress is not about comparison. It's about *witnessing growth through the eyes of the soul*. And when we anchor that witnessing in gratitude, we cultivate a sacred lens through which we view our children – not as projects to fix, but as miracles unfolding.

Gratitude, at its highest level, is a spiritual technology. It rewires the brain, softens the heart, and reorients the nervous system toward peace. When practiced intentionally, it becomes a channel for recognizing divine presence in ordinary moments[1].

Parents often get caught in the trap of waiting for "big" wins to celebrate – like a report card improvement or a successful social interaction. But what if you celebrated *process* instead of just outcomes?

What if you rejoiced over effort, connection, and presence? This shift transforms your child's environment into one of spiritual encouragement rather than silent pressure.

Start by creating a **gratitude ritual**. Each evening, pause for a moment of reflection. Ask yourself: *What did my child do today that showed courage or progress, no matter how small?* Did they try something new? Handle a change better than before? Express an emotion in a healthy way? Speak these moments aloud or write them in a journal. These seemingly small acknowledgments have enormous spiritual weight.

Children – even those with limited verbal language – feel the energy of celebration. When your face lights up, your voice warms, and your body softens in joy, your child absorbs that love. They feel seen and valued not for what they do, but for who they are becoming.

One powerful technique is the **gratitude jar**. Each family member writes down one moment of gratitude per day and places it in a jar. On challenging days, pull one out and read it together. This not only reminds you of progress but creates a visual and tactile connection to grace. It's a sacred practice that transforms discouragement into perspective.

Another beautiful practice is the **gratitude altar**. It need not be religious. Simply create a small space in your home with items that symbolize your child's growth – a photo, a stone from a calming walk, a drawing, or even a word written on paper like "Hope" or "Joy." Light a candle here once a week. Say a prayer or affirmation of thanks. Make this space a physical reminder that your family's path is a spiritual journey.

Don't forget to **include your child in the celebration**. Use whatever form of communication works for them – visuals, music, movement, or even simple shared smiles. Say things like, "I saw how brave you were today," or "Thank you for showing me something beautiful." These affirmations anchor them in the reality that *they are growing* – even when the world doesn't always understand how.

It's also essential to **reframe setbacks**. Not every day will feel celebratory. Regression happens. Emotions overflow. But even these moments hold spiritual invitations. Ask yourself, *What is being revealed here? What am I being invited to learn, or to let go of?* Then return to gratitude – not as denial, but as alignment. "Today was hard. But I'm grateful for the strength we're building."

Spiritual gratitude also includes **celebrating yourself**. You showed up. You kept going. You tried again. So often, parents feel invisible in their efforts. But every tear you've wiped, every meltdown you've managed, every appointment you've scheduled is part of a sacred offering. Pause and thank yourself. You are doing holy work.

Incorporating gratitude into milestone moments can elevate them into **sacred ceremonies**. When your child meets a goal – however small – mark it with intention. Light a candle. Say a blessing. Sing a song. Involve siblings or friends. Make the moment memorable not just through photos, but through presence.

And remember: *progress is not always visible*. Sometimes, a breakthrough is happening within your child's nervous system, their inner world, or their spiritual energy. Celebrate trust. Celebrate endurance. Celebrate being together. Gratitude doesn't demand proof – it invites perspective[2].

If you're struggling to find gratitude in a hard season, borrow someone else's. Read a story of another parent who found light in the dark. Ask a trusted friend what they see as progress in your family. Let others help you see what you've been too tired to notice[3].

Gratitude does not erase grief. It doesn't minimize struggle. But it does remind us that even in the mess, there is beauty. Even in uncertainty, there is presence. And even in the smallest steps forward, there is reason to say: *Thank you.*

When we parent with gratitude, we offer our children more than celebration – we offer them spiritual memory. One day, they'll look back and remember not just what they achieved, but how deeply they were loved while becoming.

Practical Exercise: The Daily Gratitude Mirror

Time Required: 5–10 minutes per evening

1. Place a small mirror in a quiet space.
2. Sit with your child, or alone, in front of the mirror.
3. Light a candle or take a few grounding breaths.
4. Say one thing your child did today that you are grateful for.
5. Say one thing *you* did today that you are grateful for.
6. Look into the mirror and say, "Thank you for growing."
7. End by smiling at your reflection—and your child's if present.

Repeat nightly to build emotional strength and spiritual memory.

Chapter 10: Siblings and Soul Lessons

In families raising autistic children, siblings often experience a journey that is both complex and spiritually profound. While their roles can be challenging, siblings are also uniquely positioned to grow in empathy, resilience, and emotional intelligence. Rather than viewing sibling dynamics solely through a lens of stress or sacrifice, we can reframe them as opportunities for deep soul learning – for both the autistic child and their sibling.

Every soul chooses a family for a reason. In the spiritual perspective, the sibling bond isn't random – it's divinely designed. Whether the sibling is older or younger, highly involved or more distant, there are sacred contracts at play. These relationships offer fertile ground for spiritual development, healing, and mutual transformation.

One of the most valuable soul lessons siblings learn is **compassion**. Living with a brother or sister who communicates differently, reacts unexpectedly, or requires special routines calls forth a deep level of awareness. Siblings often become sensitive to nonverbal cues, patient during transitions, and inclusive in their language and thinking[1].

Of course, this doesn't mean they never feel frustration or confusion. And that's okay. It's essential to hold space for **honest emotions**. Siblings may feel overlooked, resentful, or burdened at times. These feelings don't indicate failure – they are part of the soul's growth process. What matters is creating a home where those emotions can be safely expressed and gently guided.

One tool for supporting siblings is the practice of **reflective dialogue**. Set aside time to talk with each sibling, one-on-one. Ask open-ended questions like: *How are you feeling about things at home? What has been hard lately? What's something you wish others understood?* Listen without judgment. Validate their feelings before offering solutions. This creates emotional intimacy and teaches them that their experience matters[2].

Another powerful approach is to **affirm the sibling's unique role**. Tell them how much you appreciate their kindness, their patience, or their ability to make their sibling laugh. Celebrate their strengths not just in relation to the autistic child, but as individuals. When siblings feel seen and honored, they are more likely to embrace their role with joy rather than resentment.

Shared rituals also strengthen sibling bonds. These can be as simple as bedtime stories, shared art projects, or sibling walks in nature. Rituals build connection and offer moments of calm within the unpredictability of daily life. They remind each child that love is not only available, but abundant.

In some families, siblings become protectors or advocates. They step in during social situations, explain their sibling's behaviors to others, or help with transitions. While these traits are admirable, it's vital that the sibling doesn't feel overburdened. Make sure they know they are not responsible for managing everything. Their job is to be a brother or sister – not a second parent.

Spiritually, the sibling relationship often mirrors a **soul contract**. One child offers the challenge: the other, the response. Over time, roles may shift. The child who once struggled becomes the teacher. The sibling who was patient learns to advocate more boldly. These evolving roles are part of the sacred dance between souls learning through love[3].

Spiritual storytelling can help siblings understand their family's journey. Share the idea that every family has unique challenges and sacred strengths. Explain that their sibling came into this world with a special light – and so did they. Use metaphors, nature imagery, or even bedtime blessings to reinforce the idea that they are part of something meaningful and beautiful.

As siblings mature, their understanding of autism will evolve. Teens and young adults may wrestle with identity, responsibility, or questions about the future. Continue to hold open space for their evolving insights. Encourage journaling, counseling, or peer groups if needed. Provide books, movies, or media that affirm neurodiversity and show the power of compassionate siblinghood[4].

Also, don't underestimate the importance of **laughter**. Humor heals. Shared jokes, silly games, and playful traditions can diffuse tension and strengthen bonds. Laughter becomes a bridge between differences and a balm for difficult days.

Lastly, offer your children a vision of **spiritual equality**. Explain that while your attention may be divided in practical ways, your love is whole and sacred for each of them. Let them know that being in a family with an autistic sibling is not a limitation – it's a unique assignment filled with spiritual richness.

When you honor each child's experience, model emotional honesty, and infuse your home with love and spiritual intention, siblinghood becomes more than a dynamic – it becomes a divine classroom. The lessons learned here – compassion, resilience, advocacy, and soul awareness – will shape who your children become for the rest of their lives.

Practical Exercise: Soul Contract Journaling

Time Required: 15–20 minutes (recommended for parents, with optional sibling involvement)

1. In a journal, write your autistic child's name at the top of the page.

2. Underneath, write the name(s) of their sibling(s).

3. Reflect and write on these prompts:

    - What has each sibling taught the other?
    - What strengths do they bring to each other's lives?
    - What soul qualities are being shaped through this relationship?

4. If age-appropriate, invite siblings to write or draw their own thoughts.

5. End by writing a short blessing or affirmation for their bond.

Repeat quarterly or during significant family transitions.

_____

_____

_____

_____

_____

_____

NOTES:

Chapter 11: Planning with Peace of Mind

One of the most emotionally charged responsibilities parents face when raising an autistic child is long-term planning. Questions about future care, education, housing, and even spiritual wellbeing can feel overwhelming. Yet when approached with both faith and preparation, this process transforms from anxiety-driven speculation into a sacred act of stewardship.

From a spiritual perspective, planning ahead is not about controlling the future – it's about honoring the soul's journey by creating a container of support. When we prepare with intention, we make space for divine timing to work in harmony with practical steps. Peace of mind, in this sense, is not born from certainty, but from alignment.

The first spiritual key to peaceful planning is **clarity of vision**. Begin by asking: *What kind of life do I envision for my child when I'm no longer their primary caregiver?* This isn't just about physical needs – it's about emotional, spiritual, and relational wellbeing. Picture a setting where your child feels safe, connected, and honored for who they are. Write it down. Include not just facts, but feelings: joy, dignity, peace.

Next comes **legacy preparation**. A will or trust is not just a legal document – it's a sacred text that reflects your values, hopes, and blessings for the future. Seek an attorney familiar with special needs estate planning. Explore tools like a **special needs trust**, which allows assets to be managed for your child's benefit without jeopardizing government aid. This ensures their financial support remains intact, and that decisions align with your intentions[1].

Also consider appointing a **guardian or trustee** – not only someone who can handle logistics but someone who shares your spiritual outlook. Choose someone who sees your child not just as a responsibility, but as a soul deserving love and respect.

Another essential piece is **documenting your child's unique profile**. This can include their routines, communication style, sensory sensitivities, spiritual practices, calming techniques, and preferences. Think of it as a *"Sacred Care Manual."* Update it yearly. This becomes a loving bridge between you and future caregivers – a map of love that helps others see your child clearly.

Involve your child in planning as much as possible. For children who are verbal or use augmentative communication, ask for their thoughts. Where do they feel comfortable? What makes them feel loved? Even nonverbal children can indicate preference through behavior and energy. The goal isn't rigid decisions – it's collaboration and respect.

Community connection is another cornerstone. Identify supportive programs, housing opportunities, spiritual communities, and social networks that will remain strong in your absence. Visit these places. Meet the people. Build relationships now. The goal is continuity – not just of care, but of connection.

Create a **circle of support** – a small, trusted group of people who can check in on your child, advocate for them, and carry forward the love you've infused into their life. These may be relatives, GOD-parents, friends, clergy, or teachers. Communicate with them clearly. Hold a meeting if needed. Make it spiritual. Open with a prayer or blessing. Frame it as sacred stewardship.

Another powerful spiritual tool is the practice of **future anchoring**. Write a letter to your child, to be read when you are no longer present. In it, share your love, your memories, and your belief in their inner light. Offer words of blessing and guidance. Let them know that even when you're not physically here, your spirit walks beside them[2].

Also, prepare for **your own peace**. Facing mortality is not easy. But when you know you've taken steps to ensure your child is loved and supported, a deeper surrender becomes possible. Meditation, prayer, journaling, and talking to a spiritual advisor can help process these emotions.

Planning isn't about removing grief. It's about anchoring trust. It's saying: *I have done what I can in love. Now I release what I cannot control to the Divine.* That's faith in action.

For many parents, the most painful fear is: *Will my child be okay without me?* This question has no easy answer. But it can evolve. Over time, it becomes: *How can I build a life around my child that reflects the same love, care, and presence I've offered?* That's the invitation – to become a spiritual architect of your child's future.

Celebrate every step of this process. Every form you fill out, every phone call you make, every meeting you attend is a sacred act. It says: *You matter. Your future matters. And I will walk with you as far as I can.*

Practical Exercise: Sacred Planning Circle

Time Required: 30–60 minutes

1. Gather a small group of trusted loved ones.

2. Create a sacred space with a candle, photos, or meaningful objects.

3. Share your vision for your child's future.

4. Read aloud your child's sacred care profile (routines, joys, sensitivities).

5. Ask each person what role they can play in this journey.

6. Close with a spoken blessing over your child's life.

7. Schedule regular check-ins to revisit the plan.

_____

_____

_____

_____

_____

_____

_____

_____

_____

NOTES:

Chapter 12: You Were Chosen for This Journey

There are moments in the life of every parent of an autistic child when the weight of responsibility feels almost too heavy to bear. The therapies, the unknowns, the late nights filled with worry – all of it can bring you to your knees. But in those quiet, aching moments, a deeper truth whispers: *You were chosen for this.* Not as punishment. Not as burden. But as sacred invitation.

From a spiritual perspective, your soul and your child's soul made an agreement – a sacred contract – to walk this life path together. You were not randomly assigned. Your qualities, even those you doubt or overlook, are uniquely suited for this journey. Your capacity for growth, compassion, strength, and transformation is why you are here.

Accepting this spiritual assignment does not mean denying the difficulty. It means recognizing that within the hardship lies a hidden grace. Growth, awakening, and soul evolution often arrive disguised as challenge. By saying yes to your child, you're saying yes to your own transformation.

Many parents feel unqualified, even broken. But these feelings are often spiritual invitations. You are not being asked to be perfect – you are being asked to be *present.* To show up in love.

To grow alongside your child, not ahead of them. Your healing is part of their healing. Your awakening is a gift to your entire family.

There is no single roadmap for this journey, but there are spiritual truths that illuminate the way. One of them is the power of **presence over perfection**. What your child needs most is <u>not</u> a flawless parent but a connected one. Being fully present – emotionally, spiritually, and energetically – is one of the most healing forces on Earth[1].

Another truth is the **alchemy of love**. The love between a parent and child is a sacred crucible. Within it, fear is transmuted into trust, anxiety into wisdom, and loneliness into connection. This doesn't happen all at once. It happens one breath, one prayer, one surrender at a time.

Forgiveness plays a critical role. Not just forgiving others, but yourself. Let go of the belief that you should have done more, known more, or been more. Spiritual growth is messy. There is grace in every stumble and learning in every misstep. Offer yourself the same compassion you extend to your child.

When you remember that you were chosen, you stop comparing your life to others'. You stop looking for normal and begin seeking *meaning*. And there is deep, enduring meaning in the everyday miracles – eye contact, a moment of calm, a shared laugh, a quiet connection. These are sacred events, not small ones.

Consider your parenting role as **spiritual mentorship**. You are not just teaching life skills. You are modeling what it means to love without conditions, to rise after falling, to trust the unseen. Every time you pause instead of react, breathe instead of blame, or bless instead of judge, you are building a spiritual legacy[2].

Your child's presence in your life is not accidental – it is divinely aligned. In many ways, autistic individuals bring unique spiritual gifts: heightened perception, honesty, deep presence, and sensitivity to energy. They are often mirrors that reflect what is unhealed in us and invite us into greater awareness.

And yes, there will be days when you feel lost. Days when the therapies don't work, when professionals dismiss you, when isolation closes in. On those days, remember this truth: *You are never alone.* You are supported by an invisible network of grace. You can call upon angels, ancestors, GOD, or whatever sacred force you believe in. Prayer is not weakness – it is alignment with divine strength[3].

Spiritual resilience is cultivated through practice. Create rituals that anchor you. Light a candle before your child wakes. Say a morning prayer of strength. Keep a gratitude journal that names even the smallest blessings. These practices don't eliminate struggle, but they infuse it with meaning.

Over time, you begin to see your life not as a series of problems to solve but as a sacred curriculum. Each lesson is infused with purpose. Each challenge is a portal. And through it all, your child is not just surviving – they are teaching, loving, and transforming you.

You were chosen for this journey. That doesn't mean you always feel ready. It means the path is yours to walk, and no one else could walk it in the way you do. Your journey is holy. Your parenting is prayer. Your family is not broken – it's breaking open into something deeper.

Practical Exercise: Mirror of Purpose

Time Required: 10–15 minutes

1. Find a mirror and a quiet space.

2. Look into your own eyes and say aloud:

   - *"I am not perfect, but I am present."*
   - *"I was chosen for this journey."*
   - *"My child's soul and my soul are walking this path together in sacred trust."*

3. After each affirmation, breathe deeply.

4. Write in a journal: *What am I learning from my child? What is my soul being invited to remember?*

5. Close with a short prayer, blessing, or moment of silence.

Repeat as needed – especially on difficult days.

_____

_____

_____

_____

_____

_____

_____

_____

NOTES:

SECTION TWO:
For Support Professionals

Theme: Soul-Centered Service, Compassionate Practice, and Holistic Understanding

For educators, therapists, clinicians, and social workers, this section provides a spiritual lens for working with autistic individuals. By viewing clients as whole beings—mind, body, and spirit—support professionals can enhance their practice with compassion, sensitivity, and deeper respect. These chapters offer frameworks for creating spiritually safe environments, supporting communication beyond words, and ethically empowering those you serve. Whether you're in a classroom, clinic, or home, you'll find insight and inspiration to guide your service with integrity and heart.

NOTES:

Chapter 13: Seeing the Individual Beyond the Label

Labels can be useful tools in clinical settings – helping professionals access resources, coordinate care, and offer targeted support. Yet from a spiritual perspective, the label of "autism" is just one small part of a much larger truth: each autistic individual is a soul with a unique purpose, gifts, and essence. The danger lies not in using a label, but in letting that label become a limit.

As a support professional – whether teacher, therapist, clinician, or social worker – you are invited to look beyond diagnosis codes and standardized treatment plans. You are being called to see the full, sacred person before you. This is not a denial of science or best practices – it's an expansion. It's a commitment to holistic, soul-centered service.

The first spiritual principle in this approach is **person-first presence**. When you sit across from someone, take a moment to center yourself. Quiet your inner noise. Ask silently: *Who is this being before me? What wisdom do they carry? What does their energy communicate beyond their words?* In doing so, you shift from problem-solving to connection-building.

Seeing the individual beyond the label also means releasing the temptation to compare. No two autistic individuals are the same. While certain support strategies may be helpful across many profiles, a spiritually informed professional recognizes the uniqueness of each person's neurotype, life story, trauma history, and soul path[1].

Language matters. The way we speak about autistic individuals shapes how we relate to them. Avoid deficit-based terms that define a person by what they "lack" or "struggle with." Instead, use language that reflects capability, humanity, and dignity. For example, rather than saying someone is "low-functioning," describe their support needs and their strengths. Say, *"They benefit from daily structure and have a remarkable memory for detail."*

Another spiritual cornerstone is **non-verbal honoring**. Some of the most powerful communication comes without words – through energy, body language, presence, and even silence. When a client rocks, stims, or avoids eye contact, don't rush to "correct." Instead, observe with curiosity and respect. Ask: *What is being expressed? What need is this behavior meeting?* Often, the behavior is the communication.

Deep listening is a sacred act. It requires more than hearing words – it asks for attunement. This means noticing shifts in tone, posture, energy. It means allowing space for expression in all forms, including AAC (augmentative and alternative communication), gestures, art, movement, and ritual.

In spiritually grounded practice, the professional is not the fixer but the facilitator. Your job is not to mold the person into "normal," but to nurture their potential, honor their pace, and create environments where they can thrive as themselves.

This approach requires **humility**. Professionals must be willing to unlearn as much as they learn. The autistic experience cannot be fully understood through textbooks alone – it must be informed by autistic voices. Read books and articles by autistic self-advocates. Watch their videos. Attend their workshops. They are not just clients; they are collaborators, teachers, and guides[2].

Spiritually attuned professionals also practice **energetic hygiene**. Before entering a session, ground yourself. Clear your energy field. Set an intention to serve with clarity and compassion. Many autistic individuals are sensitive to energy, and your emotional state affects them. When you show up regulated, they feel safer.

Create environments that respect both **sensory needs** and **spiritual dignity**. This could mean adjusting lighting, reducing noise, or allowing movement during sessions. But it also means treating every person as inherently whole – worthy of time, respect, and patience.

One profound practice is **soul witnessing**. Take a moment during your session – perhaps at the beginning or end – to silently affirm the sacred nature of the person you're serving. Say inwardly: *I see your light. I honor your path. I walk beside you in service, not above you in authority.*

Over time, this way of seeing becomes a way of being. You'll begin to notice shifts: deeper trust with clients, more intuitive responses, and a renewed sense of purpose in your work. Clients may not articulate it, but they'll feel the difference. They'll feel seen – not just assessed. They'll feel welcomed – not just accommodated.

This chapter is not an invitation to abandon protocols or clinical excellence. Rather, it's a reminder to bring heart and spirit into the equation. When we lead with soul, we do more than support – we uplift. We don't just document progress – we bear witness to sacred transformation.

You are not just a professional. You are a guide, a companion, and at times, a sacred mirror. The label may open the door – but it is your presence that invites true healing.

Practical Exercise: Soul-Witnessing Protocol

Time Required: 5–10 minutes before a session

1. Sit quietly before meeting with your client.
2. Close your eyes and take three grounding breaths.
3. Visualize your client surrounded by light.
4. Inwardly affirm:
   - *"This person is a soul with wisdom and purpose."*
   - *"I release all assumptions."*
   - *"I am here to witness, not fix."*
5. Open your session with calm, centered presence.
6. Repeat after the session to reflect and give thanks.

_____
_____
_____
_____
_____
_____
_____
_____
_____

NOTES:

Chapter 14: Creating Sensory- and Spirit-Friendly Spaces

A truly inclusive space honors both the **sensory needs** and the **spiritual essence** of the person within it. For autistic individuals, the environment is more than a backdrop – it can be a source of safety or distress, calm or chaos, connection or withdrawal. As a support professional, your ability to create sensory- and spirit-friendly spaces directly impacts the well-being of those you serve.

Start with the core principle: **Environment is energy.** Every room carries a vibration shaped by its lighting, sound, layout, and emotional tone. A spiritually aware practitioner doesn't just furnish a space - they *prepare* it, energetically and physically, to welcome the whole person.

Lighting plays a powerful role. Fluorescent lights, common in schools and clinics, often flicker at frequencies that can agitate the nervous system. Whenever possible, use natural light or warm-toned, dimmable lighting. Allow access to sunglasses, hats, or hooded sweatshirts for those who are light-sensitive. This isn't a disruption – it's a form of self-regulation[1].

Sound sensitivity is another common sensory experience. Spaces should allow for quiet zones or the use of noise-canceling headphones.

Soft, predictable background noise (like a low hum or soft instrumental music) may be soothing to some, while overstimulating to others. Ask each person about their preference.

Smell is often overlooked but deeply impactful. Avoid strong perfumes, cleaning products with heavy fragrance, or diffusers unless the scent is chosen collaboratively. Scents like lavender or cedarwood may support grounding – but always ask before introducing new sensory stimuli.

Seating and spacing also matter. Some individuals prefer soft chairs that allow movement; others thrive with upright, structured seating. Whenever possible, offer choice. The ability to choose where and how to sit gives individuals a sense of control – critical for nervous system safety.

Incorporate **regulation tools** into your environment: fidget items, weighted blankets, textured fabrics, calming visuals, and space for stimming without judgment. What may seem like distractions to the untrained eye are often sacred tools of balance for the autistic nervous system.

Spiritual inclusivity is just as vital. Consider the energetic tone of your space. Is it chaotic or calm? Is there a visible symbol of peace – like a plant, candle, sacred image, or grounding object? These elements speak to the spirit, not just the senses.

Even your **personal presence** affects the energy of the room. Take a moment to ground yourself before sessions. Walk in slowly. Smile gently. Speak with warmth and clarity. Your nervous system becomes a co-regulator. In many ways, *you* are the most important part of the space.

Designing sensory and spirit-friendly environments is not about perfection – it's about **intentionality**. Ask yourself before each session:

- What does this person need to feel safe?
- Is there too much stimulation in this room?
- How can I co-create a sense of peace, presence, and belonging?

This also requires **flexibility**. What works for one person may not work for another. Being willing to adjust lighting, tone, furniture, or your own posture shows deep respect for the individual. It tells them: *You matter here.*

Honor **ritual and routine** as spiritual anchors. Begin sessions the same way – a grounding breath, a question, a moment of silence. End with the same consistency. These rhythms create containers of safety that allow the soul to come forward[2].

Some professionals choose to create **spiritual sensory corners** – small, designated areas where individuals can retreat when overwhelmed. These spaces might include calming lights, images of nature, a soft rug, a mirror, prayer beads, or a spiritual affirmation card. It's a sacred pause in a chaotic world.

It's also helpful to involve the client in shaping the space. Ask:

- What colors feel calming to you?

- Do you want music or silence?

- Would you like a plant, crystal, or soft item nearby?

Empowering choice invites trust and deeper engagement. It tells the individual: *This is not just my space – it's ours.*

The more spiritually inclusive your space, the more powerful the healing. A classroom, therapy room, or clinic doesn't have to feel clinical. It can feel like sanctuary. It can be a sacred container where learning and transformation happen not *in spite* of sensory needs but *through* honoring them.

Creating these spaces doesn't require a large budget – it requires a large heart. The autistic soul is sensitive, wise, and often energetically attuned. When we honor that truth, we shift from caretaking to communion.

Let every room you design, enter, or hold become a spiritual offering – an altar of peace, permission, and possibility.

Practical Exercise: Sacred Space Assessment

Time Required: 15–20 minutes

1. Walk through your therapy, classroom, or office space.

2. Observe lighting, noise levels, seating, smells, and emotional tone.

3. Ask:

    - What in this space might overstimulate?
    - What supports regulation and peace?
    - Is there space for quiet retreat or spiritual reflection?

4. Make a list of 3–5 small changes you can make.

5. Implement one change this week and observe any shifts in your clients' responses.

_____

_____

_____

_____

_____

_____

_____

NOTES:

Chapter 15: Holistic Communication Tools

Communication is more than language. It is energy, intention, and sacred connection. For autistic individuals, communication often unfolds through alternative means – gestures, sounds, devices, images, behavior, and presence. As a spiritually aware professional, your role is not to "fix" communication but to *expand* your understanding of how the soul expresses itself.

Traditional models often focus on helping the autistic person meet neurotypical communication standards. But holistic communication turns that approach on its head. It asks: *How can we meet them where they are? How can we honor all forms of expression as sacred, valid, and complete?*

Holistic communication integrates physical, emotional, and spiritual awareness. It involves:

- Respecting alternative communication forms (AAC, behavior, art)

- Recognizing the energetic message behind the words – or the silence

- Creating a space where every mode of expression is welcome

Augmentative and Alternative Communication (AAC) is not a last resort – it's a legitimate language system. Whether it's a speech device, picture exchange cards, a whiteboard, or sign language, AAC can unlock connection. Celebrate every attempt at expression. Be patient. Wait. Allow time. Rushing or interrupting silences can unintentionally send the message that only spoken language has value[1].

Sometimes, behavior *is* communication. A child who refuses to enter a room may be saying, *"This space overwhelms me."* A client who suddenly melts down may be expressing, *"I'm past my limit."* Step back and ask: *What is this soul trying to tell me?* This practice transforms frustration into compassion.

Energetic listening is a vital tool. It means tuning in to the space between words – the tone, the posture, the emotional vibration. It requires presence and intuition. Before reacting, ask inwardly: *What am I feeling in their field? What does their energy say, even if their mouth does not?*

Rituals of communication can bring comfort. Begin each session with a predictable routine: a greeting card, a calming sound, a symbolic object. These anchor the client in trust. Consistent closing rituals – such as saying goodbye with a wave, placing a hand on the heart, or using a goodbye symbol – create a sense of completion and respect.

Visual tools are powerful. Many autistic individuals process visual information more easily than auditory. Use charts, photos, color-coded schedules, feeling thermometers, or image boards. These support understanding while reducing overwhelm.

Movement and rhythm are often overlooked as communication tools. Rocking, dancing, or repetitive hand motions can all carry emotional content. Honor these movements as sacred expression. If appropriate, invite movement-based communication into your sessions – swaying, tapping, or using rhythm instruments.

Remember that communication includes **self-expression** – not just conveying needs, but sharing feelings, preferences, creativity, and identity. Offer opportunities for journaling, drawing, storytelling, or spiritual ritual. These open channels to the soul.

When challenges arise – silence, scripting, echolalia – don't interpret them as obstacles. Silence may be a boundary. Scripting may be a bridge. **Echolalia** (repeating phrases) may be a processing tool. Ask: *What is the deeper purpose of this form?* Assume competence. Assume meaning. Assume presence.

Your own presence is a communication tool. When you enter a room regulated and spiritually grounded, you communicate safety. When you listen with your whole being, you say: *"I see you."* This kind of communication transcends language – it is soul-to-soul.

Incorporate **sacred listening** practices into your work. Slow down. Use eye contact when appropriate – but never force it. Allow quiet pauses. Let the client guide the pace. Listen not only to reply, but to witness.

Above all, affirm that communication is a birthright – not a privilege earned by meeting certain criteria. Every human being has the right to be heard; in the way they are able to speak.

As you implement holistic tools, you'll begin to notice a softening in the space. Clients may open up in surprising ways. They'll sense that they don't have to mask or perform. They'll feel honored. And in that honoring, deeper healing begins.

You're not just helping someone communicate. You're helping them reclaim their voice – and in many cases, their soul's right to be known.

Practical Exercise: The 3-Level Listening Practice

Time Required: 10–15 minutes (during or between sessions)

1. Choose a session or moment to practice.

2. Level 1 – *Literal Listening*: What are the words being used? What do they mean on the surface?

3. Level 2 – *Emotional Listening*: What feeling is present behind the words (or silence)?

4. Level 3 – *Spiritual Listening*: What deeper message or need is the soul communicating?

5. After the session, journal your insights. Reflect on how it changed your response.

6. Repeat weekly to strengthen your sacred listening muscles.

_____

_____

_____

_____

_____

_____

NOTES:

Chapter 16: Being Trauma-Informed and Spiritually-Aware

Trauma-informed Care is essential when working with autistic individuals – but to truly serve the whole being, it must be paired with spiritual awareness. Being trauma-informed means recognizing the signs of trauma and understanding its widespread impact. Being spiritually-aware means seeing each individual not just as someone shaped by pain, but as a sacred soul on a journey of healing and transformation.

Many autistic individuals have experienced trauma, both directly and indirectly. This includes sensory overwhelm, bullying, restraint, exclusion, constant misunderstanding, and the pressure to mask their true selves. Even the well-intentioned demands of behavior-based therapy models can feel invasive or invalidating when not aligned with the individual's internal experience[1].

Trauma can affect:

- Regulation and emotional expression
- Trust in others, especially authority figures
- The nervous system's ability to rest, learn, and connect

Professionals must move beyond the question, *"What's wrong with them?"* to ask, *"What happened to them – and how can I offer safety now?"*

Safety is not only physical – it is **emotional, energetic, and spiritual**. To create it:

- Avoid sudden changes in routine
- Respect personal boundaries and consent
- Explain what's happening and what's next
- Allow breaks, silence, and self-regulation without shame
- Avoid touch without permission – even supportive gestures

Spiritual awareness deepens this work. It honors the person's inner light and affirms their wholeness, even if they have experienced deep wounding. A spiritually-aware trauma-informed approach recognizes that healing does not mean erasing pain but integrating it into a deeper sense of self.

Energetic sensitivity is common in autistic individuals and can heighten the trauma response. Loud environments, chaotic emotions from others, or overly clinical settings can feel overwhelming. Create **sanctuary spaces** that are calm, quiet, and energetically grounded. Bring your own presence into balance before engaging.

Adopt a posture of **sacred witnessing**. Let your presence say: *"I see your pain, and I will not look away."* Validate the individual's emotional experience without trying to fix it. Sometimes the deepest healing comes from being lovingly held in our truth.

Narrative safety is also important. Allow clients to tell their story in their own time and way – whether through speech, art, movement, or silence. Resist imposing your own story on theirs. Invite them to co-create a new story – one in which they are resilient, valued, and spiritually guided.

Avoid spiritual bypassing – the tendency to dismiss pain with spiritual platitudes like *"Everything happens for a reason."* While spiritual meaning can arise from suffering, it must be discovered by the individual, not imposed by others.

Grounding rituals support trauma recovery. Gentle breathwork, visualizations of light, calming mantras, nature contact, and the use of sacred objects (stones, candles, textures) can help clients anchor into the present moment. Always offer – not require – such tools.

Your own spiritual awareness is part of the healing field. Reflect on your energy before a session. Are you calm? Judgment-free? Open-hearted? Trauma-informed practice includes the practitioner's inner work. Healing flows most freely when you are present, attuned, and spiritually grounded[2].

Collaboration with caregivers is key. Help parents and family members understand trauma responses and how to support healing at home. Model compassion and patience. Encourage rituals of reassurance and moments of connection.

One of the most sacred gifts you can offer is **consistency**. Inconsistent care can feel like betrayal. Predictable rhythms – same time, same space, same welcoming greeting – build trust. Trust is the soil in which transformation grows.

Affirm the individual's **spiritual autonomy**. Ask what brings them comfort. Invite their spiritual preferences, whether that means prayer, nature, art, silence, or music. Never assume belief – always ask. Spiritual awareness is not conversion – it's compassion.

Remember: you are not here to "heal" someone in the sense of fixing them. You are here to walk beside them in dignity, presence, and love. The soul often heals not through intervention, but through relationship.

When trauma is met with spiritual presence, the nervous system begins to relax. The individual feels seen, not analyzed. Heard, not evaluated. Loved, not managed. And in this sacred space, the soul breathes freely.

Practical Exercise: The Sacred Space Checklist

Time Required: 10 minutes (before each session)

1. Breathe deeply three times to center yourself.

2. Ask silently: *"Am I calm and grounded right now?"*

3. Check the environment: Is the space peaceful, uncluttered, sensory-respectful?

4. Prepare a sacred object (stone, candle, texture, or meaningful image) for grounding if needed.

5. Ask inwardly: *"Can I hold space today without needing to fix?"*

6. Say silently: *"I honor this soul's path. I offer my presence, not perfection."*

Use this checklist before every client interaction to align trauma-informed skills with spiritual awareness.

_____

_____

_____

_____

_____

_____

NOTES:

Chapter 17: Recognizing Spiritual Intelligence

Spiritual intelligence is often overlooked in clinical and educational settings. Yet for many autistic individuals, spirituality is not only present – it is profoundly alive. Spiritual intelligence refers to the ability to perceive, understand, and connect with a reality beyond the material. It includes intuition, deep empathy, awareness of patterns, ethical clarity, and a sense of life purpose. When we expand our lens to include spiritual intelligence, we can begin to see our autistic clients and students in a wholly new light.

Many autistic individuals demonstrate qualities that align with high spiritual intelligence:

- Profound curiosity about the cosmos, nature, or metaphysical topics
- Deep moral or ethical reasoning beyond their years
- A strong sense of justice and fairness
- Heightened sensitivity to emotional and energetic environments
- Repetitive behaviors that mirror meditative or ritualistic practices

- Nonlinear communication that reveals symbolic or intuitive insight¹

Traditional assessments may miss or misinterpret these traits. A child staring at leaves fluttering in the wind may not be "distracted," but *deeply attuned*. A teenager scripting lines from a movie may be echoing a spiritual message embedded in that scene. A young adult who avoids social chatter might be quietly contemplating life's bigger questions.

As professionals, we must ask: *Are we seeing the full being before us? Or are we reducing them to a diagnosis?*

Spiritual intelligence expresses differently for everyone. Some may find it through religion or prayer. Others through art, nature, music, silence, or even systems like astrology or numerology. Some may not name it at all but still live in profound connection with the unseen.

Creating space for spiritual intelligence in your work does not mean imposing beliefs. It means staying open. It means affirming that autistic individuals are not spiritually broken, delayed, or less evolved. They may in fact be more attuned to spiritual realms than we expect.

The challenge is this: how do we recognize spiritual intelligence without pathologizing (to view or characterize as medically or psychologically abnormal) it?

Here are signs to look for:

- **Existential questioning:** Asking about life, death, meaning, or the universe
- **Spontaneous empathy:** Deep compassion for animals, people, or even inanimate objects
- **Symbolic communication:** Using metaphor, art, or image to convey inner truths
- **Unusual presence:** A calm, wise, or otherworldly quality that defies age or context
- **Spiritual language:** Speaking about light, energy, soul, God, or love naturally and unprompted[2]

Spiritual intelligence often coexists with sensory sensitivities. The more attuned one is to energy, the more intense both beauty and overwhelm can be. A bright light, loud sound, or crowded room may not just be "too much" – it may interfere with subtle spiritual perception.

To honor this, create spaces and practices that validate the spiritual. Invite your clients to:

- Share dreams or imaginative visions
- Describe how different environments feel energetically
- Explore sacred symbols, stories, or practices that resonate with them

- Use visual or creative expression to explore inner states

Avoid interpreting these insights as fantasy or avoidance. Validate the inner experience. When someone shares a vision of light, a conversation with a tree, or a feeling that they "came from the stars," meet it with curiosity, not correction.

Offer tools that support spiritual expression: nature walks, ritual objects, calming music, drawing mandalas, lighting a candle, or silent meditation. Don't assume everyone will want these – but make them available.

Your **presence** is part of the invitation. When you listen without judgment, when you slow down and respect the sacred in someone's words or silence, you help spiritual intelligence unfold.

Spiritual intelligence does not depend on cognitive ability. Non-speaking individuals may demonstrate profound spiritual awareness through gaze, gesture, vibration, or energy. Don't equate lack of speech with lack of soul.

If you're unsure how to begin, try asking simple, open-ended questions:

- *What makes you feel peaceful inside?*
- *Do you ever think about where you came from?*
- *What colors or shapes feel special to you?*

- *Is there a word or sound that makes you feel strong or happy?*

Allow the answers to emerge without pressure. Some may not respond with word – but their energy, expression, or posture may shift. That is communication.

One of the most healing acts you can offer is **spiritual witnessing** – the practice of seeing the sacred in another without needing proof or explanation.

When we stop assuming spiritual immaturity based on diagnosis, we unlock the potential for deeper healing, greater trust, and richer connection. We stop seeing our clients as cases to manage – and begin seeing them as souls to honor.

Practical Exercise: Spiritual Intelligence Reflection Sheet

Time Required: 10–20 minutes

1. Reflect on one client, student, or autistic individual you work with.

2. Ask yourself:

    - Have I noticed signs of spiritual intelligence?
    - How do they express wonder, ethics, empathy, or energy?
    - Have I validated or dismissed these expressions?

3. Write down 3 ways you can support their spiritual development.

4. Choose one way and begin implementing it this week.

5. At week's end, journal how your relationship with the individual may have shifted.

_____
_____
_____
_____
_____
_____
_____

Chapter 18: Serving the Family as a Whole

Support professionals often focus on the individual autistic person – and while this is crucial, true healing and empowerment occur when the _entire_ family system is engaged. Autism doesn't exist in isolation. It weaves itself into the daily rhythms, emotions, and spiritual lessons of the whole household. To offer spiritually aware support, we must recognize and honor the sacred interdependence of the family unit.

Each family is a unique constellation. Some are overwhelmed and seeking clarity. Others are hopeful but exhausted. Some carry deep spiritual faith; others feel disconnected from any spiritual path. Your role is not to prescribe a single way – but to become a steady, open-hearted presence that encourages healing across all levels: emotional, practical, relational, and spiritual.

Start by listening – _deeply_. Each family member has a story. The autistic individual, of course, but also the siblings, parents, guardians, and even extended family members who may carry unspoken concerns or burdens. A spiritually attuned professional listens beneath the words. What is being held in silence? What grief, joy, confusion, or wisdom lives in the space between?

When you meet with families, begin with grounding. Invite a moment of quiet breath. Ask how everyone is doing – not just the one in services. Normalize the idea that the entire family deserves support. This simple act can shift the tone from a problem-solving meeting to a sacred circle of care.

Offer **relational reflections** – mirroring back strengths you observe in how the family interacts. For example: "I notice how gently your son touches your hand when he's overwhelmed – that's a beautiful way of self-regulating through connection." This reminds families of what *is* working, not just what's challenging.

Parents often carry guilt. Some feel they didn't catch the signs "soon enough." Others question every decision they've made. Spiritually grounded professionals create a judgment-free space where forgiveness, compassion, and acceptance can unfold. Remind them: *You are growing alongside your child.*

Siblings, too, need sacred attention. They may feel protective, resentful, proud, left out, or confused. Invite them to share their experience. Use art, storytelling, or play if language is difficult. Affirm that their role is important – but they are not expected to be caretakers. They are children, too, with their own spiritual path.

Rituals of connection can transform chaotic family dynamics. Encourage families to create daily or weekly rhythms that bring everyone together – lighting a candle at dinner, saying three things they're grateful for, taking a nature walk on weekends, or using music to reset after tough days. These don't have to be perfect. **The goal is *presence*, not performance.**

Teach families to recognize **spiritual cues** within their dynamics. A child who hides under blankets may be seeking energetic rest. A sibling who hums the same song may be regulating through sound. A parent who starts meditating every morning may be anchoring the energy for the entire household.

Help families reframe challenges as opportunities for sacred growth. Instead of: "My child is so rigid with routine," shift to: "Our family is learning the spiritual practice of structure and stability." Instead of: "We're always tired," try: "We're being invited into deeper self-care and communal compassion."

Language matters. Model spiritually inclusive, non-pathologizing speech:

- "Let's support this sensitivity" vs. "Let's fix this behavior"
- "This is a soul strength in disguise" vs. "This is a deficit"
- "How can we help the family regulate together?" vs. "How do we get them to comply?"

When possible, include **spiritual or cultural practices** that are meaningful to the family. Ask: *Are there rituals, prayers, songs, or traditions you'd like to bring into this process?* Let their answers guide the rhythm of your sessions.

For families without a spiritual framework, offer universal tools: breathwork, gratitude journaling, nature connection, kindness rituals, and moments of stillness. These transcend belief systems while fostering spiritual wellness.

Above all, invite the family to see themselves as a team – not perfect, but sacredly connected. When one person struggles, the others are not enemies or rescuers. They are companions. When one person grows, the others are not left behind – they are uplifted.

True family-centered support includes the **energy of the home**. Is it chaotic or calm? Overstimulating or balanced? You can't control what happens behind closed doors, but you can offer suggestions: decluttering a shared space, adding calming sensory objects, establishing clear routines, or creating a designated "peace corner."[1]

Be aware of your own expectations. Not every family will adopt your suggestions. That's okay. Your job is not to transform them, but to witness them with love, and offer guidance rooted in trust.

Over time, the family may begin to notice a shift. They'll speak more gently. Laugh more freely. Regulate more quickly. And above all, they'll begin to see one another not as burdens to be managed – but as souls growing together.[2]

Practical Exercise: Family Energy Mapping

Time Required: 20–30 minutes (can be done in session or at home)

1. On a large sheet of paper, draw the family as a constellation – each member is a star.

2. Use lines or symbols to represent energy flow: calm, tension, support, confusion, joy.

3. Let each person (if possible) add to the map.

4. Reflect together:
   - Where is the energy strong or weak?
   - Where do we feel connection or distance?
   - What rituals or actions could balance the flow?

5. Revisit the map over time as dynamics evolve.

_____

_____

_____

_____

_____

_____

Chapter 19: Guiding with Meaning and Purpose

Every human being carries within them a longing to live with purpose. For autistic individuals, that sense of purpose may not always align with traditional expectations – but it exists nonetheless, and honoring it is essential to spiritual empowerment. As a support professional, you have the sacred responsibility of helping the individuals you serve uncover, express, and live in alignment with their soul's unique direction.

Purpose is not about productivity or conforming to societal milestones. It is about meaning. It is about honoring the passions, joys, and inner drives that bring a person to life. For autistic individuals, these may include a deep connection to nature, a fascination with numbers, an ability to comfort others, or a profound artistic gift. Our job is not to shape their path but to walk beside them as they discover it for themselves.

Start by observing without judgment. What patterns do you see in their play, their focus, or their energy? Does a client consistently organize objects in a way that reveals a sense of order or visual design? Do they show emotional intelligence through how they respond to others' moods? Pay attention to what lights them up – it's often a window into their calling.

Engage in open-ended inquiry. Ask them, "What do you love?" or "What makes you feel calm or strong?" If verbal expression is limited, use drawing, objects, or movement to invite answers. Even silence has meaning – sometimes presence itself is the message.

Support professionals must balance **encouragement with reverence**. It's easy to push toward skill-building goals for the sake of job readiness or independence. But spiritual guidance asks: *Is this task aligned with their deeper self?* Will this build confidence and wholeness, or simply compliance?

Use strengths-based language in your assessments and reports. Say, "This individual thrives in structured environments where their attention to detail shines" rather than "struggles with flexibility." Or "expresses care through small daily routines" instead of "fixated on sameness." Framing matters.[1]

Help create environments that support spiritual flourishing. This might mean:

- Providing sensory-friendly zones for quiet reflection
- Offering flexible schedules that allow for internal rhythms
- Incorporating nature, art, or music into daily programming
- Giving permission for nonverbal communication as valid and whole

Meaning and purpose are often reflected in **ritual and rhythm**. A client who insists on greeting everyone with the same phrase may be offering a sacred blessing. One who walks the perimeter of a room before settling may be spiritually "preparing" the space. When we see these not as obstacles but as expressions of being, our support becomes exponentially more respectful and empowering.

Families and team members should be included in these conversations. Help them shift from deficit-based thinking to spiritual curiosity. Invite them to consider:

- What brings this person joy?
- What activities seem to restore their energy?
- What causes stress or internal resistance?
- When do they feel most seen and safe?

Use storytelling to help connect the dots. For example: "I notice that every time she finishes her drawing, she smiles and taps her pencil three times. That might be more than a habit – it could be her way of sealing her creation with pride or intention."

Affirm that spiritual purpose doesn't always lead to a job title. Some may find purpose in routine, presence, caregiving, art, learning, or even silence. For those who desire employment or vocational growth, align their role with their nature. Don't force square pegs into round holes.

Offer consistent opportunities for **soul-aligned choice-making**. Ask: "Do you want to do this now or later?" or "Would you rather work here or there?" This cultivates agency and self-trust.[2]

Honor moments of spiritual growth even when they don't show up on a data sheet. The first time a client makes eye contact with soft eyes, initiates a touch of comfort, or expresses frustration without meltdown – these are sacred milestones. Recognize them.

Be patient. Purpose unfolds over time. Sometimes you'll help someone discover a love of gardening, or that their deep empathy makes them a natural companion to animals. Other times, you'll simply offer presence and consistency so they feel safe enough to bloom.

Above all, reflect back to every client: *Your life matters. Your presence matters. You are not broken or behind – you are on a sacred journey, and I am honored to walk beside you.*

Practical Exercise: The Purpose Discovery Journal

Time Required: 15 minutes daily for one week

1. Create a simple 3-column journal page with the headings: "What did I enjoy today?" / "What made me feel calm or proud?" / "What did I avoid or dislike?"

2. Invite the individual (with support if needed) to fill in the page each day.

3. Use pictures, symbols, colors, or words based on communication style.

4. After 7 days, review together. What patterns are visible?

5. Reflect on how these insights can shape future routines, goals, or environments.

_____
_____
_____
_____
_____
_____
_____
_____

NOTES:

Chapter 20: Sacred Structure and Routines

For autistic individuals, structure and routine are not just tools for organization – they are spiritual lifelines. Far from being rigid or limiting, sacred structure provides safety, continuity, and a rhythm that allows the nervous system and the soul to rest. As support professionals, it is our task to help create, honor, and adjust routines in ways that reflect both spiritual integrity and practical function.

Autistic individuals often experience the world with heightened sensitivity – physically, emotionally, and energetically. In a world filled with unpredictable stimuli, routines act as grounding anchors. They foster a sense of control and predictability, which leads to reduced anxiety and greater self-trust.[1]

Routines can be misunderstood. Some may view them as compulsive or inflexible. But from a spiritual lens, repetition and ritual have always held power. Monks chant daily. Indigenous communities follow seasonal cycles. Families light candles on holidays. Predictability creates space for presence.

Support professionals can bring this sacredness into everyday routines by helping clients design rhythms that align with their natural flow. This may involve:

- A morning ritual that starts with soft lighting and quiet music

- A predictable sequence for transitions between tasks

- Visual schedules that offer gentle, consistent cues

- A sacred wind-down ritual before sleep, such as guided breathing or storytelling

It is important to match the level of structure to the individual's needs. For some, highly specific routines offer deep peace. For others, too much rigidity increases anxiety. The key is **collaborative calibration** – observing, listening, and adjusting as needed.

Structure is not just for time management; it supports emotional regulation. For instance, knowing what comes next can help an individual prepare mentally and energetically, reducing meltdowns or shutdowns.[2] A consistent lunch routine, for example, might include sitting in the same spot, using preferred utensils, and playing familiar calming music.

Support professionals can assist families and teams in creating routines that are spiritual, not sterile. Ask:

- What makes this moment sacred?

- What sensory or emotional needs are present at this time of day?

- How can this routine promote connection rather than compliance?

For example, instead of framing brushing teeth as a chore, encourage it as a "blessing of the body." Use affirming language: "Let's care for your body because it's precious." Over time, this reframing supports not just participation, but self-worth.

Introduce **rituals of rhythm** – short, consistent practices that mark transitions or hold meaning. These might include:

- Lighting a candle before starting homework
- Saying a short affirmation before meals
- Pausing for breathwork after school or therapy
- Using an essential oil to signal bedtime

These rituals do not need to be elaborate. The consistency is what transforms them into something sacred.

Use tools that support structure:

- **Visual Schedules** (pictures or symbols for steps)
- **Timers** (for transitions)
- **Checklists** (for building independence)
- **Calendars or planners** (for those who read)

Honor the individual's role in designing their structure. Ask:

- "What helps you feel calm in the morning?"
- "What order do you like to do things in?"

- "How can we make this part of the day feel better?"

For clients with limited verbal communication, observe closely. Which tasks do they resist or gravitate toward? What time of day do they seem most energized or peaceful?

Spiritual awareness reminds us that **all routines are relational**. They are never just about tasks. They are about connection – to the self, to others, to space, and to time.

Guide teams and families to reflect:

- Is our morning routine rushed or reverent?
- Do our transitions feel chaotic or clear?
- Are we offering enough recovery time between activities?

Offer grace when routines falter. Life is unpredictable. Illness, travel, school closures, and emotional states all affect rhythm. The goal is not perfection, but adaptability rooted in love.

You can teach families the **Sacred Routine Reflection**:

1. What part of our routine feels peaceful?
2. What part feels stressful?
3. What one small shift could help?

Encourage documentation of routines with flexibility built in. A good visual schedule may include:

- Core activities (e.g., breakfast, therapy, rest)

- Choice spaces (free play, quiet time)
- Visual indicators for changes (a "change card" or soft chime)

Avoid using routines as tools of control. Instead, co-create them as agreements of trust. Let the routine serve the person – not the other way around.

Finally, remember that you, too, benefit from sacred structure. Your presence, your consistency, and your calm create the energetic foundation that allows clients to feel safe. Your routines of reflection, preparation, and self-care enable you to serve from a full cup.

Practical Exercise: The Sacred Routine Builder

Time Required: 20–30 minutes (with client or caregiver)

1. Create a daily chart with 3 columns: Time / Activity / Energy Level
2. Fill in current routines as observed or reported.
3. Circle parts of the day that feel calm or joyful.
4. Underline parts of the day that feel tense or rushed.
5. For one challenging time block, co-create a new micro-routine (e.g., add a sensory break, change order of tasks).
6. Repeat weekly and adjust as needed.

_____

_____

_____

_____

_____

_____

_____

_____

Chapter 21: Mindfulness and Grounding Practices

In a world that often feels overwhelming to autistic individuals, mindfulness and grounding are not luxuries – they are lifelines. These practices support nervous system regulation, emotional resilience, and a sense of internal safety. For support professionals, integrating these tools into daily routines is both a spiritual and therapeutic gift.

Mindfulness is not about clearing the mind or sitting still. At its core, mindfulness is the act of **paying attention with compassion**. It allows individuals to connect with their present-moment experience without judgment. This can be transformative for autistic clients, many of whom experience sensory overload, emotional flooding, or social fatigue.[1]

Grounding, on the other hand, helps reestablish a connection to the body and to the physical world. It is especially useful during moments of anxiety, dissociation, or dysregulation. Grounding can involve touch, movement, breath, or sensory input.

For support professionals, the first step is modeling calm presence. When your voice, body language, and energy communicate steadiness, it sends a message: *You are safe here. I'm not rushing you. I am with you.*

Begin each session with a grounding moment:

- A few deep breaths with the client
- Naming one thing you each see, hear, and feel
- Gently pressing feet to the floor together

Even 30 seconds of mindful presence can reset the tone of a session.

Tailor practices to each individual's needs and preferences. Examples include:

- **Breathwork** (e.g., "Smell the flower, blow out the candle")
- **Weighted blankets or lap pads** for physical grounding
- **Hand tracing** or tactile objects (e.g., smooth stones, fidget tools)
- **Movement-based grounding** such as rocking, stretching, or pacing
- **Sensory mindfulness** – noticing textures, smells, or sounds without judgment

Mindfulness does not always look quiet. Some clients may benefit from **active mindfulness**, like coloring mandalas, watering plants, stacking stones, or engaging in repetitive motion.[2]

Use visual supports. Create a "Mindful Moment" choice board with pictures of options (e.g., listen to music, take deep breaths, hold a warm object). Empower the individual to choose what feels good.

Consider establishing rituals:

- A breathing exercise before transitions
- A grounding practice before and after therapy
- A centering moment before group work or community outings

Invite spiritual reflection without imposing beliefs. You might say:

- "What helps you feel calm on the inside?"
- "What feels strong in your body today?"
- "Can you feel your feet on the ground like a tree with roots?"

Offer these questions gently and respect non-responses. Presence is enough.

Use storytelling to introduce mindfulness. Share short narratives like:

"There was once a boy who felt like his brain was a racecar. When he closed his eyes and listened to his breath, it helped the racecar slow down."

Adapt practices to energy levels. For high-energy states, offer movement-based grounding (e.g., bouncing a ball, stomping feet, jumping on a trampoline). For low-energy or shutdown states, offer calming tactile input or gentle rocking.

Teach co-regulation. Invite the individual to mirror your breathing or movements. Say, "Let's do this together."

Model emotional labeling. Use phrases like:

- "My body feels tight – maybe I'm nervous."
- "That sound surprised me. Let's take a breath."

This normalizes emotional awareness and promotes emotional literacy.

Help families and teams integrate mindfulness at home or school:

- A morning breathing game
- A calming song after transitions
- A grounding basket with soft items, chewables, or essential oils

Train others to see mindfulness as a tool for connection – not just behavior management.

Recognize moments of mindfulness in your clients. Reflect back:

- "You noticed your hands were tight and you shook them out. That was wise."
- "You sat with your feelings instead of walking away. That was strong."

Remember, mindfulness is not about compliance. It's about connection – to self, to body, and to the present.

When practiced consistently, mindfulness and grounding cultivate inner peace, stronger self-regulation, and a more centered way of being in the world. As a professional guide, your calm presence and sacred intention can make this possible.

Practical Exercise: The 5-Senses Grounding Walk

Time Required: 10–15 minutes

1. Take a short walk indoors or outdoors with the client.

2. Pause at intervals and ask:

    - "What's one thing you see?"
    - "What's one thing you hear?"
    - "What's one thing you feel?"
    - "What's one thing you smell?"
    - "What's one thing you can taste (or imagine tasting)?"

3. Reflect together: "Which sense helped you feel calm?"

4. End the walk with 3 slow breaths and optional gentle stretching.

_____
_____
_____
_____
_____
_____
_____

Chapter 22: Developing Sacred Rapport

Sacred rapport is the deep, soulful connection between support professionals and autistic individuals that transcends clinical roles and creates a space of genuine safety, trust, and mutual presence. It's not built on authority or diagnosis, but on authentic being-with. For autistic individuals – who may have experienced repeated misunderstandings, sensory overwhelm, or social disconnection – this level of connection can be profoundly healing.

Unlike traditional rapport, sacred rapport emphasizes intuitive alignment, spiritual respect, and energetic safety. It invites us to go beyond the checklist of professional empathy and embrace the sacred responsibility of bearing witness to another's full humanity.[1]

To build sacred rapport, support professionals must first cultivate self-awareness. Your presence is your first tool. Are you grounded? Are you listening beneath the words? Are you attuned not just to behaviors but to the soul beneath them?

Autistic individuals often pick up on subtle energies and unspoken dynamics. They may respond not to what is said, but to the emotional tone behind it. This is why authenticity is key. If you are calm, sincere, and accepting, that inner truth will come through.

Sacred rapport is relational, not transactional. It develops slowly, through:

- Consistent presence
- Emotional honesty
- Deep listening
- Respect for boundaries and preferences
- Co-regulation instead of control

Simple, repeated gestures build trust: saying hello with warmth, using the same greeting ritual, honoring silence, and maintaining nonjudgmental eye contact (or avoiding it if preferred).

Being present without pressure is one of the greatest gifts you can give. Sometimes, that means sitting in shared quiet. Other times, it means following their lead – literally and metaphorically.

A child may prefer parallel play before interaction. An adult may test your reliability through silence or small challenges. Sacred rapport asks us to meet them where they are – not where we want them to be.

Language matters. Use strength-based, inclusive terms. Avoid deficit-based descriptions or overly clinical jargon. Instead of saying, "He's noncompliant," try, "He's expressing a boundary." Instead of "She's refusing to engage," say, "She's choosing space right now."

Respect sensory preferences. Rapport often grows faster when environments feel safe. Offer noise-canceling headphones, reduce harsh lighting, or allow for movement and fidgeting. These small accommodations speak volumes: *You matter. Your comfort matters.*

Ritual also plays a key role in rapport. A song that begins each session, a handshake, or a mantra like "We're a team" can become anchoring symbols of relationship.

Offer choices. Sacred rapport honors autonomy. Ask:

- "Would you like to talk now or sit quietly?"
- "Do you want the blue or green marker?"
- "Should we work at the table or on the floor?"

These micro-moments of control empower clients and build respect.

Pay attention to transitions. Goodbyes are often as important as hellos. Ritualize them: a shared phrase ("See you next time!"), a visual calendar, or a gentle reminder.

When rupture occurs – and it will – repair it. Sacred rapport does not mean perfect connection. It means being willing to return with humility and love. Say:

- "I'm sorry I missed what you needed."
- "Can we try again?"

- "You matter to me."

Parents and caregivers can also be included in rapport-building. Share insights, listen to their wisdom, and form a united circle of support. Let them know: this is not just a service – it's a relationship.

Sacred rapport also allows for moments of joy and celebration. Laugh together. Notice the sparkle in their eye when they achieve something. Mirror their excitement. These shared emotions create spiritual intimacy.

Importantly, do not conflate rapport with over-involvement. Boundaries are essential. Sacred rapport thrives in relationships where clarity, consent, and mutual respect guide every step.

As support professionals, take time to reflect:

- How do I cultivate trust without pressure?
- How do I repair when mis-attunement happens?
- Do I see this person's soul or just their behavior?

Your willingness to build sacred rapport is not just professional – it's transformational. It holds the potential to restore trust, renew dignity, and awaken connection in lives that may have longed for it.

Practical Exercise: The Rapport Reflection Journal

Time Required: 10–15 minutes after each session

1. After a session, reflect and journal your answers to the following:

    - Did I meet this person with full presence?
    - How did they respond emotionally and energetically?
    - Was there a moment of connection? Describe it.
    - Was there a moment of disconnection? How can I repair it?
    - What sensory, emotional, or spiritual needs seemed to arise?

2. Review these weekly to track growth and adjust your approach.

_____

_____

_____

_____

_____

_____

_____

_____

NOTES:

Chapter 23: Ethical Empowerment

True empowerment is not about control – it's about liberation. Ethical empowerment invites support professionals to shift their role from manager to mentor, from authority to ally. In the context of autism, this means we must center autonomy, consent, dignity, and self-expression, all while honoring the sacred nature of each individual's path[1].

Many traditional systems of care are built on a foundation of compliance. Autistic individuals are often encouraged to mask behaviors, suppress sensory needs, or meet arbitrary social milestones. Ethical empowerment challenges this paradigm. It asks: **What does the individual want, need, and value – and how can we support that without overriding their agency?**

From Compliance to Consent

Empowerment begins with a conscious move from demanding compliance to fostering consent. Instead of "Let's get through your to-do list," try, "What do you feel ready for today?" Empowerment asks permission, not forgiveness. It trusts the individual's capacity to lead – even when support is needed.

Ask:

- "How do you want to begin?"
- "Would you like help with this, or would you prefer space?"

- "Can we talk about what works for you?"

Even non-speaking individuals can communicate consent and preference through AAC (augmentative and alternative communication), gesture, eye gaze, or affective behavior [2]. As professionals, we must learn to listen in all those languages.

Collaboration Over Control

Ethical empowerment is a collaborative process. It's not about guiding someone *your* way – it's about co-creating a path together. Whether it's working on a classroom accommodation, therapy goal, or home routine, the individual should always be part of the conversation.

Ask:

- "How does this feel to you?"
- "Would you change anything?"
- "Do you want to try it differently next time?"

This empowers not only choice, but *voice*. The more we invite feedback, the more we communicate respect. Respect strengthens trust, and trust is the foundation of ethical rapport.

Empowerment Is Spiritual

The core of ethical empowerment is reverence. We're not just helping a person – we're honoring a soul. That means creating space for the individual's spiritual identity, belief system, and inner world to unfold and be expressed.

Ask reflective questions like:

- "What helps you feel peaceful?"
- "Who or what gives you strength?"
- "What makes you feel proud?"

These moments go beyond the clinical – they create sacred connections rooted in human dignity.

Avoiding Saviorism

In ethical empowerment, professionals resist the urge to "save" or "fix." Saviorism appears as over-accommodation, speaking *for* instead of *with*, or rescuing when the individual might have been able to succeed with support. When we empower ethically, we walk beside – not in front.

Instead of:

- "Let me handle this for you."

Try:

- "Would you like a strategy or want to try first on your own?"

Independence isn't the absence of help – it's the presence of choice.[3]

Supporting Self-Advocacy

Ethical empowerment teaches and models self-advocacy. This includes:

- Encouraging individuals to say "no" safely and confidently
- Practicing role-plays with self-advocacy language
- Supporting access to advocacy communities and resources

Give phrases like:

- "I need more time."
- "I'm not comfortable with that."
- "Can we do this differently?"

These are not just skills – they are spiritual affirmations of personal worth and agency.

Inclusive Environments

An empowered individual thrives in a supportive environment.

This includes:

- Providing access to communication tools (AAC devices, whiteboards, visuals)
- Allowing movement and sensory tools without judgment
- Displaying affirming artwork, messages, and sensory-friendly layouts

Let your physical and relational environment say: "You belong here."

The Ethics of Empowerment

Regularly reflect:

- Am I honoring this person's voice and pace?
- Am I giving choices or just instructions?
- Am I listening more than I speak?

The ethics of empowerment is not just professional – it's personal. It calls us to hold our power responsibly, remain open to feedback, and walk the talk of love-in-action.

Practical Exercise: The Empowerment Check-In

Time Required: 10–15 minutes

Purpose: Reflect on your daily interactions with clients or students.

Instructions:

1. Recall a recent session or moment with an autistic individual.

2. Write down 3 things you said or did that invited choice or autonomy.

3. Write down 2 things you could shift next time to improve consent, collaboration, or self-advocacy.

4. Finish with this affirmation:
   "I choose to empower with humility, honor, and care."

_____

_____

_____

_____

_____

_____

_____

Chapter 24: Caring for the Whole Being

In a world of diagnoses, checklists, and service plans, it's easy to forget that we are not supporting a disorder – we are supporting a **whole being**. Caring for an autistic individual means acknowledging and honoring every layer of their humanity: mind, body, emotions, and spirit.[1] This chapter calls support professionals to move beyond a reductionist lens and toward holistic, compassionate care.

Wholeness Over Fragmentation

Traditional care often focuses on what's "wrong" – the deficits, the challenges, the behaviors to be fixed. But ethical and spiritual service requires a shift: from **fragmentation to wholeness**. Each individual is already whole, not because they meet a neurotypical mold, but because their humanity and spirit are inherently sacred.

Rather than asking, *"What's missing?"*, begin asking:

- *"What's present and powerful?"*
- *"What part of this individual longs to be seen, nurtured, or affirmed?"*

Every person has emotional needs, energetic rhythms, inner truths, and sacred dignity. To care holistically is to recognize and honor them all.

Integrating Mind, Body, Spirit, and Emotion

1. **Mind**

    Autistic individuals often have powerful cognitive gifts – deep focus, unique memory patterns, strong logic, and profound insight. Support should nurture mental growth while respecting neurological differences. Avoid overstimulation. Respect information-processing time. Offer meaningful challenges rooted in curiosity rather than pressure.

2. **Body**

    Sensory and physical experiences vary greatly. Respect individual needs related to touch, movement, sound, and personal space. Support regulation with:

- Body breaks

- Movement tools

- Restorative positioning

- Access to food and hydration that honors dietary preferences

The body is a temple – and often a messenger. Observe how physical states mirror emotional truths.

3. **Emotions**

    Rather than suppressing emotions, allow space for their full expression. Meltdowns are not misbehavior; they're emotional overload. Create emotional safety by:

- Remaining calm
- Avoiding sudden stimuli
- Affirming the individual's experience with phrases like:
    - "It's okay to feel upset."
    - "You're safe with me."

Model emotional literacy and self-regulation. Help name emotions with visuals, storyboards, or gentle conversation.

4. **Spirit**

    The spiritual dimension is often ignored in professional practice – but it is vital. Ask yourself:

- What brings this person peace?
- Do they connect with nature, music, prayer, or ritual?
- What gives them joy or a sense of purpose?

Spiritual care is not about imposing beliefs. It's about **honoring the inner landscape** of meaning, connection, and sacred worth.

Relationship-Centered Care

Caring for the whole being requires a **relationship-centered** approach. Procedures and interventions matter, but relationship is what transforms. Be fully present. See beyond the diagnosis. Use soft eyes. Show up with reverence.

Build relational safety by:

- Consistently affirming strengths
- Avoiding judgmental language
- Asking before touching or adjusting
- Listening beyond words

Whole-person care asks us to show up as whole people too.

Co-Regulation and Energetic Exchange

All human interactions involve **energy**. As a support professional, your energy – calm, chaotic, anxious, grounded – affects the individual you serve.[2] Co-regulation is the process of helping someone regulate by offering steady, compassionate presence.

When a person is distressed, offer:

- Calm breathing
- Silence

- Nonverbal cues of safety (open posture, soft tone)

Sometimes doing less is doing more. Your presence may be the healing tool.

Respecting Identity and Inner Truth

Wholeness means respecting **who the person is** – not just what they can do. This includes:

- Gender identity
- Cultural heritage
- Communication preferences
- Neurodivergent expressions (e.g., stimming, scripting, echolalia)

Celebrate these as aspects of soul expression, not symptoms to manage.

Use affirming language:

- "You're allowed to be fully you."
- "Your voice matters in every form it takes."

Creating Whole-Person Support Environments

Caring for the whole being extends to physical and relational settings:

- **Design:** Use calm lighting, quiet zones, and flexible furniture

- **Language:** Choose words that uplift, not diminish
- **Programs:** Include mindfulness, creative expression, social rituals, and movement opportunities

Support plans should include:

- Emotional wellness goals
- Sensory accommodations
- Preferred spiritual practices or values (when applicable)
- Relationship goals rooted in connection, not correction

Holistic Care is Sacred Service

Supporting the whole being is not about doing more tasks. It's about showing up more **intentionally**, **consciously**, and **respectfully**. It's a spiritual act. It says:

- *You are not broken.*
- *You are not alone.*
- *You are not your diagnosis.*
- *You are whole, holy, and worthy of love.*

Practical Exercise: Whole-Person Reflection Grid

Time Required: 10–15 minutes

Purpose: To deepen your awareness of the individual's complete needs.

1. Draw a grid with four columns labeled: Mind, Body, Emotions, Spirit.

2. Under each, write observations about the person you support:

    - What brings them joy?
    - What triggers overwhelm?
    - How do they connect with others or themselves?

3. Add 1–2 new ideas per column that could support that domain holistically.

4. Keep the grid visible during planning or support sessions.

_____

_____

_____

_____

_____

_____

NOTES:

SECTION THREE:
For Autism Advocates

Theme: Spiritual Justice, Inclusion, and Dignity for All

Advocacy is not just about changing policy – it's about healing hearts, lifting voices, and restoring sacred worth to those who have been misunderstood or marginalized. This section speaks to those who work to make the world more inclusive and conscious. Whether you are an autistic self-advocate, family member, faith leader, or community organizer, these chapters offer a spiritually infused roadmap for bringing about change. Through justice, empathy, and soul-first vision, you'll learn to champion neurodiversity as a sacred gift and call others into the light of compassionate awareness.

NOTES:

Chapter 25: The Spiritual Power of Neurodiversity

Neurodiversity is more than a scientific concept – it is a **spiritual truth**. It reminds us that humanity is not meant to be uniform but beautifully varied. When we view autism and other neurological differences through a spiritual lens, we begin to see not deficits, but design – sacred, intentional, and purposeful.[1]

Neurodiversity as a Sacred Gift

The neurodiversity paradigm affirms that neurological differences such as autism, ADHD, dyslexia, and more are natural variations of the human experience. From a spiritual perspective, these differences are not mistakes. They are part of a divine blueprint that reflects the complexity, creativity, and consciousness of life itself.[2]

Autistic individuals often experience the world in profound ways – feeling, sensing, and perceiving reality on frequencies many others overlook. Their unique patterns of thought and behavior can be seen as spiritual gifts:

- Deep focus = meditative presence
- Scripting = sacred repetition
- Stimming = energetic regulation
- Silence = soulful reflection

Rather than resisting these expressions, we can **reverence** them.

Ancient Wisdom and Neurodivergent Minds

Across history, societies have often misunderstood those who perceive differently. Yet ancient wisdom traditions speak of seers, prophets, healers, and dreamers – people set apart because of their sensitivity, insight, or connection to realms beyond the physical. Is it possible that many of these spiritual figures were neurodivergent?

The autistic mind may not filter the world the same way as the neurotypical one. It often absorbs more sensory data, processes information non-linearly, and focuses with extraordinary depth. These traits align closely with spiritual attunement.

To recognize neurodivergence as sacred is to **break the cycle of pathologizing difference** and to open space for honoring divine diversity.

The Soul's Journey Through a Neurodivergent Lens

From a metaphysical viewpoint, we might consider that each soul chooses their life path – including the challenges, gifts, and identity they will carry. If that is true, then neurodivergent individuals are not anomalies. They are **purposeful participants in a much larger spiritual ecosystem**.

This view allows us to shift how we interpret difference:

- A child who avoids eye contact is not "deficient" – they are preserving energetic boundaries.
- A teen who scripts dialogue may be practicing a sacred form of vocal grounding.
- An adult who doesn't conform to societal expectations may be modeling divine authenticity.

Rather than correcting these behaviors, we are invited to **witness them as expressions of the soul's journey**.

Community as a Reflection of Divine Interdependence

Every society needs a diversity of roles, perspectives, and insights. Neurodivergent individuals expand a community's range of awareness, compassion, and innovation. In the spiritual ecology of humanity, every soul contributes to the whole – like organs in a body, or instruments in a symphony.

Neurodivergence invites us to examine and soften our attachments to what is "normal," "appropriate," or "correct." It challenges ego and awakens heart-centered living. It reminds us that love is not about sameness – it is about **connection across difference**.

Spiritual Strengths in Neurodivergent Individuals

Many autistic people exhibit spiritual sensitivities that are often overlooked:

- A strong sense of justice and truth

- Deep empathy (sometimes misinterpreted due to expression)
- Intense connection to nature, animals, or music
- Capacity for stillness, silence, or single-pointed focus
- Spiritual questions and inner philosophical life at a young age

These qualities can become powerful spiritual anchors when recognized and nurtured.

A Call to Spiritual Inclusion

For families, educators, spiritual leaders, and advocates, embracing neurodiversity as a spiritual principle means:

- Creating spaces of belonging, not just accommodation
- Using inclusive liturgy, language, and rituals
- Teaching that all minds are divine, even if they communicate differently
- Celebrating neurodivergent stories, saints, prophets, and leaders

When spiritual communities become inclusive of all neurologies, they become more **human**, more **sacred**, and more aligned with universal truth.

Practical Exercise: The Neurodiversity Blessing Practice

Time Required: 10 minutes

Purpose: To transform perception through intentional spiritual language.

Instructions:

1. Think of a neurodivergent person you support, love, or know.

2. Write a blessing that affirms their uniqueness using sacred language. Example:

   - "Your mind is a temple of insight."
   - "You are a divine expression of difference."
   - "Your rhythm is a sacred beat in the song of life."

3. Speak or write this blessing regularly. Allow it to reshape how you see them – and how they see themselves.

_____

_____

_____

_____

_____

_____

_____

NOTES:

Chapter 26: Centering Autistic Voices

In a world that often speaks over, about, or around autistic individuals, there is a revolutionary spiritual act that transforms everything: **listening**. Centering autistic voices is not simply a matter of inclusion – it is an act of justice, reverence, and sacred realignment.[1]

When we center autistic perspectives, we don't just change policies or programs. We change paradigms. We shift from *doing things for* to *being in relationship with*. From *interpreting behavior* to *honoring communication*. From *assuming needs* to *respecting truths*.

This chapter calls all support professionals, advocates, and spiritual leaders to become **amplifiers, not translators** – to lift up autistic voices in their own form, rhythm, and truth.

Why Centering Matters

Autistic people have long been left out of the conversations and decisions that affect their lives. The result … Misrepresentation, underrepresentation, and harm. Policies are made without consultation. Therapies are designed without collaboration. Assumptions become the architecture of entire systems.

Centering autistic voices means correcting this imbalance by saying:

- "Your experience is valid."
- "Your story matters."
- "We are here to learn from you."

When you center a voice, you **decentralize your own**. You listen more. You pause longer. You ask before interpreting.

Listening Across Differences

Not all autistic people communicate the same way and not all communication looks like speech. Listening means:

- Paying attention to behavior, body language, and silence
- Valuing AAC (augmentative and alternative communication) tools
- Resisting the urge to reframe or "translate" for neurotypical comfort
- Accepting emotional honesty without judgment

Listen not for what makes sense to you – listen for what makes sense to *them*.

From Tokenism to True Partnership

Including one autistic voice in a meeting is not the same as centering autistic leadership. Tokenism checks a box. Partnership builds trust.

Ask:

- Are autistic people leading this discussion?
- Are we co-creating solutions or just collecting feedback?
- Are we acting on what is shared?

Respect is demonstrated not in hearing – but in **responding**.

Making Space for All Forms of Voice

Centering voice means honoring all communication forms:

- Spoken words
- Typed thoughts
- Art and creativity
- Movement and energy
- Silence, presence, and being

Don't mistake non-speaking for non-knowing. Assume competence. Always.

As one AAC user wrote:

"I type, therefore I am." ²

Let the method of expression never matter more than the message.

Language That Honors

Part of centering autistic voices is respecting how autistic people describe themselves. Many prefer identity-first language ("autistic person" rather than "person with autism") as it reflects pride, not shame. Others may choose otherwise. The point is: **ask and follow**.

Avoid deficit-based terms like:

- "Low-functioning"
- "Burden"
- "Suffer from autism"

Choose language that uplifts:

- "Autistic individual"
- "Neurodivergent communicator"
- "Support needs" (rather than functioning labels)

Words create worlds. Speak with reverence.

Making Platforms Sacred

Every system – whether a school, church, clinic, or community center – has a platform. Use that platform to center autistic wisdom. Invite autistic speakers, authors, artists, and leaders. Feature their books in your libraries, their quotes in your sermons, their insights in your trainings.

Remember: if you're speaking about autism and no autistic people are present, something is missing.

The Sacredness of Story

When autistic people share their stories, they're not just recounting facts. They're sharing *soul*. These stories carry truth, pain, resilience, and insight. Receiving them is a sacred act.

Treat these moments with:

- Presence
- Patience
- Gratitude
- Action

The storyteller does not owe you comfort, clarity, or cohesion. They owe you nothing. You owe them **respect**.

Humility Is a Spiritual Discipline

Centering autistic voices requires humility – the ability to be corrected, to let go of assumptions, to sit with discomfort. It is not our job to agree or approve. It is our job to listen, learn, and let go of control.

Ask yourself regularly:

- Am I making space or taking space?
- Am I leading or following?
- Am I lifting voices or replacing them with my own?

True advocacy requires stepping aside so others can step forward.

Practical Exercise: The Listening Commitment

Time Required: 10 minutes

Purpose: To reflect on your role in elevating autistic voices.

Instructions:

1. Write the names of 3 autistic individuals whose voices you have recently read, heard, or learned from.
2. Reflect: How did their perspective shift or challenge your thinking?
3. Write 2 specific actions you can take to center autistic voices more consistently in your life or work.

Say this aloud:
"I commit to listening more deeply, honoring more fully, and amplifying more faithfully."

_____

_____

_____

_____

_____

_____

_____

NOTES:

Chapter 27: Dignity for All

Dignity is not a reward – it is a right. It does not need to be earned through behavior, productivity, or communication style. Every person, regardless of neurotype, age, or ability, is inherently worthy of respect, safety, and honor.[1]

When we truly believe that everything about our systems, relationships, and support strategies changes.

The Spiritual Core of Dignity

To recognize human dignity is to acknowledge the sacredness of the soul. In spiritual traditions around the world, this idea is foundational: that every human being is created in the image of the divine, carries a piece of the infinite, or is woven from the same spiritual thread.

Dignity, then, is not just about human rights. It is about **spiritual truth**. And when we deny dignity to someone, we are denying the divine within them.

Autistic individuals – especially those who communicate, behave, or experience the world differently – are often subjected to environments and attitudes that erode dignity:

- Being spoken over or about, rather than with
- Being touched without consent

- Being forced into compliance
- Being denied choice, space, or silence

These actions, while often unintentional, are violations of dignity. And they harm the spirit.

Dignity Is Not Conditional

One of the most harmful myths in support systems is that dignity must be earned through cooperation, "appropriate" behavior, or perceived intelligence.

But dignity is **unconditional**. It belongs to the person who scripts instead of speaks, the one who rocks in public, the one who cannot make eye contact, the one who melts down in distress. Their dignity is intact – even if others do not see it.

Our job as professionals and advocates is to see that dignity clearly and protect it fiercely.

Small Moments, Sacred Impact

Dignity is upheld (or undermined) in the smallest moments:

- Do you knock before entering a person's space?
- Do you ask for consent before offering support?
- Do you speak directly to the individual, not just their parent or support person?

- Do you allow someone to stim or self-soothe without interruption?

These acts may seem minor, but they carry **spiritual weight**. They send the message: *You matter. Your body is your own. Your voice is heard. Your presence is sacred.*

Language That Honors

Words can affirm or erode dignity. Be mindful of how you speak about autistic individuals – especially in professional reports, public discussions, or interdisciplinary meetings.

Instead of:

- "Non-compliant" → Try: "Expressing boundaries"
- "Manipulative" → Try: "Seeking control in a disempowering environment"
- "Low-functioning" → Try: "Has higher support needs"

Dignity-affirming language reflects trust, not suspicion. Curiosity, not criticism. Respect, not pity.

Respecting Emotional Sovereignty

Emotional expression – whether quiet or intense – is personal. Allow individuals to express their inner states without judgment or suppression. Do not shame tears, meltdowns, monotone speech, or repetitive phrases. These are ways of being, not flaws to be corrected.

Support with compassion:

- "It's okay to feel overwhelmed."
- "Take the time you need."
- "I'm here when you're ready."

This is how we uphold emotional dignity.

Dignity in Advocacy and Policy

At a structural level, dignity must be the foundation of all systems that touch autistic lives – education, healthcare, faith communities, justice systems, and public spaces.

Policies should:

- Prioritize consent and choice
- Include autistic leadership in design
- Eliminate restraint and seclusion
- Fund inclusive and affirming services
- Train staff in trauma-informed, neurodiversity-affirming approaches

Dignity is not a side issue. It is the *soul* of ethical service.

A Culture of Dignity

Creating a culture of dignity means making it the **default posture**. It is not a technique – it is a way of being. In every interaction, ask:

- Am I listening with respect?
- Am I offering choice and consent?
- Am I interpreting through a lens of compassion?

Let your tone, body language, and presence communicate this silent but powerful truth: *You are safe. You are honored. You belong.*

Practical Exercise: The Dignity Audit

Time Required: 10–15 minutes

Purpose: To reflect on how your environment and practices uphold dignity.

Instructions:

1. Think of a recent interaction with an autistic individual.

2. Write down 3 things you did or said that supported their dignity.

3. Write down 2 moments that could have unintentionally disrespected their autonomy or identity.

4. For each, write a new phrase, behavior, or mindset that would honor dignity more clearly next time.

5. Post a reminder in your space: *Dignity is sacred. Lead with it.*

_____

_____

_____

_____

_____

Chapter 28: Creating Sacred Inclusion

Inclusion is not simply about allowing someone to be present. It is about **making room for the soul** – welcoming the full person, as they are, with reverence, respect, and celebration. Sacred inclusion means going beyond tolerance to embodiment, beyond awareness to love.[1]

Inclusion becomes sacred when it reflects the spiritual principle that **all people are divine expressions** of a shared source. When applied to neurodiversity, sacred inclusion means not only inviting autistic individuals into society's spaces – but reshaping those spaces to reflect their presence, power, and perspective.

Inclusion That Heals, Not Just Hosts

Many environments claim inclusion but fall short of actual belonging. An autistic individual may be present in a classroom, faith group, or workplace – but excluded from decision-making, cultural resonance, or authentic participation.

Sacred inclusion requires **transformation**, not tokenism:

- Transformation of environments: making them sensory-friendly, communication-flexible, and trauma-aware

- Transformation of attitudes: moving from pity to partnership, from stereotype to soul-recognition

- Transformation of systems: involving autistic individuals in every stage of planning and leadership

This is not about doing a favor. It is about correcting a **spiritual imbalance** – and co-creating justice through design.

Building Spiritually Inclusive Spaces

Every space, from therapy rooms to sanctuaries, carries spiritual energy. How can we ensure autistic individuals feel safe, welcome, and honored in them?

Key practices:

- **Environmental Respect:** Provide quiet zones, visual supports, soft lighting, and options for sensory regulation.

- **Communication Accessibility:** Include AAC devices, allow scripting, slow the pace, and practice patient listening.

- **Cultural Representation:** Use materials, language, and images that reflect neurodiverse identities as sacred and powerful.

- **Relational Inclusion:** Foster real relationships where autistic people are equals, not recipients.

Ask: *Does this space feel safe for a non-speaking autistic child? For a sensory-sensitive adult? For an autistic elder with deep spiritual questions?*

If not, change it.

The Role of Faith Communities

Spiritual institutions often unintentionally exclude neurodivergent individuals by adhering to rigid traditions, silent expectations, or overstimulating environments. But faith communities can become **beacons of sacred inclusion** when they commit to transformation.

Examples of inclusive faith practices:

- Quiet worship areas or services for neurodivergent individuals

- Spiritual education that includes neurodiverse teachers, stories, and themes

- Clergy training in autism awareness and spiritual communication differences

- Rituals that allow movement, stimming, or silence without shame

Spirituality is for everyone. Sacred inclusion makes that truth visible.

From "Special Needs" to "Shared Humanity"

Labeling autistic individuals as having "special needs" can sometimes reinforce separateness. Sacred inclusion reframes support as **mutual growth**.

What do autistic people bring to the community?

- Deep perception
- Unfiltered truth
- Creative insights
- Loyal presence
- Soulful silence

Instead of focusing on how to "accommodate" autistic people, shift to asking: *How do we become more human by including them?*

Inclusion as Relationship

At its heart, inclusion is not a policy. It is a relationship. Sacred inclusion honors the spiritual truth that we belong to each other – not despite our differences, but **through them**.

To practice this:

- Build long-term, mutual relationships with autistic individuals
- Learn how they experience inclusion –

not just what you think it should look like

- Invite them into leadership, storytelling, and spiritual expression

Inclusion that is not mutual becomes charity. Inclusion that is mutual becomes **communion**.

Reflecting on Power

Inclusion must come with a conscious reckoning of power. Who sets the rules of the space? Who determines who is "welcome"? Who defines what is "appropriate"?

To create sacred inclusion:

- Share power by inviting autistic input in design and leadership
- Examine and challenge internalized biases
- Be willing to unlearn and re-learn in community

Only then can inclusion move from symbolic to **spiritually embodied**.

Celebrating Diverse Expressions of the Sacred

Sacred inclusion means expanding our definition of spiritual presence. An autistic person flapping during prayer may be worshiping. A non-speaking teen humming during reflection may be anchoring. A child scripting scripture may be communing with Spirit.

Celebrate:

- Movement
- Repetition
- Silence
- Directness
- Deep focus

These are not deviations from sacredness – they **are sacredness in motion**.

Practical Exercise: The Sacred Inclusion Checklist

Time Required: 10–12 minutes

Purpose: To assess the inclusivity of your personal, spiritual, or professional space.

Instructions:

1. Choose a setting you oversee (e.g., classroom, sanctuary, counseling room).

2. Ask:

    - Are there flexible seating and lighting options?
    - Are AAC and visual supports available?
    - Are autistic individuals visible in artwork, leadership, or storytelling?
    - Are staff/volunteers trained in neurodiversity awareness?
    - Are behaviors like stimming accepted without correction?

3. Score each area 1–5. Reflect on one step you will take to increase sacred inclusion this month.

Post this affirmation: *"This is a space of dignity, difference, and divine belonging."*

_____

_____

_____

NOTES:

Chapter 29: Educating with Love and Light

Education is far more than academics – it is the **awakening of the soul**, the nurturing of potential, and the fostering of connection. For autistic individuals, education can either be a place of wounding and misunderstanding or a sanctuary of empowerment and light.[1]

Educating with love and light means grounding learning environments in **empathy, spiritual awareness, and unconditional respect**. It means teaching not to fix or normalize – but to inspire, affirm, and illuminate the path of each learner.

Love Is the Foundation

To educate with love is to teach from the heart and for the heart. Love in education is not soft or permissive – it is **strong, wise, and courageous**. It calls us to meet the child or adult in front of us not with judgment, but with reverence.

Love-centered educators:

- See beyond the diagnosis to the whole soul
- Value curiosity over compliance
- Seek connection before correction

- Recognize that all behavior is communication

Every child deserves to walk into a learning space and feel: *"I am safe here. I am seen. I belong."*

Light Is the Guide

Light symbolizes awareness, clarity, and truth. To educate with light is to seek understanding – not just of content, but of the learner's essence. It's choosing to illuminate possibilities instead of casting shadows of doubt or fear.

Light-based education includes:

- Honoring different learning styles, paces, and rhythms
- Providing multi-sensory approaches and calm environments
- Making space for silence, stillness, and processing
- Being transparent, consistent, and emotionally available

In this light, even the quietest or most unconventional learner can **shine**.

The Spiritual Role of the Educator

Educators are not merely instructors – they are **soul stewards**. Whether in a classroom, therapy room, homeschool, or community space, those who teach are called to hold sacred space for growth.

The spiritual educator:

- Models patience and presence
- Encourages inner exploration as much as outer achievement
- Practices humility and ongoing reflection
- Protects the learner's dignity at all costs

Every interaction is an opportunity to uplift or diminish. Choose always to uplift.

Creating Spiritually Safe Classrooms

A spiritually safe classroom is a sanctuary where learners feel emotionally, physically, and energetically protected.

To build such a space:

- Greet each student with intentional presence
- Respect sensory sensitivities (lighting, noise, textures)
- Use predictable routines balanced with flexibility
- Offer quiet zones and movement options
- Display affirming language and imagery that reflect neurodiversity and belonging

Let every element of the space say: *"Your soul is welcome here."*

Teaching the Whole Person

Autistic learners often have needs beyond cognitive instruction. They may require spiritual grounding, emotional regulation, or sensory nourishment. A whole-person approach to education embraces **mind, body, spirit, and heart**.

Support learners by:

- Teaching breathwork or grounding exercises
- Incorporating nature, music, or art as spiritual tools
- Offering rituals that promote peace, such as morning blessings or gratitude circles
- Respecting solitude as a form of restoration, not withdrawal

These aren't extras. They're essentials. They invite the soul to feel safe enough to emerge.

Consent, Choice, and Voice

Empowering education centers student **voice and autonomy**. This is especially vital for autistic learners, who are often forced into compliance-based systems.

Model respect by:

- Asking before touching or redirecting
- Providing options and choices throughout the day

- Encouraging all forms of expression (AAC, movement, scripting)
- Validating emotions instead of policing them

Love and light flourish where control diminishes and collaboration grows.

From Curriculum to Calling

Education is not only about what is taught – it's about **why**. A spiritually infused curriculum includes academic goals, yes – but also:

- Emotional intelligence
- Purpose discovery
- Compassionate communication
- Self-awareness and inner resilience

Ask: *"Does this lesson feed the soul? Does it offer tools for a meaningful life?"*

True education helps each student remember who they are – **and why they matter**.

Blessings for Educators

Let this be your mantra:

> "May I teach with compassion.
> May I listen with humility.
> May I guide with light.
> May I love without condition."

You are not just educating minds. You are awakening **divine potential**.

Practical Exercise: Soul-Centered Lesson Reflection

Time Required: 10 minutes

Purpose: To align your teaching with love and light.

Instructions:

1. Think of a lesson, activity, or session you recently facilitated.

2. Ask:

    - Did I approach it with presence and care?
    - Did I allow for student choice or voice?
    - Did I honor spiritual or emotional needs?

3. Write one thing you'd do differently next time to more deeply embody love or light.

4. Bless your teaching space with this phrase: *"Let this be a place of wisdom, warmth, and wonder."*

_____

_____

_____

_____

_____

_____

NOTES:

Chapter 30: Language That Honors the Soul

Words are more than tools for communication – they are vessels of spirit. Language has the power to heal or harm, to uplift or diminish, to illuminate the soul or obscure it. For autistic individuals, language often becomes the battleground where dignity, identity, and acceptance are either protected or violated.[1]

To honor the soul, we must speak with reverence. We must choose language that reflects not just what a person does, but **who they are in their wholeness**. This chapter invites us to re-examine the words we use and the beliefs they carry, with the goal of cultivating speech that affirms sacred worth.

The Spiritual Weight of Language

Every word carries energy. When we describe someone as "high-functioning," "non-compliant," or "low-verbal," we are not simply using labels – we are broadcasting judgments. Even well-meaning phrases like "special needs" or "disordered" can subtly imply deficit, brokenness, or exclusion.

From a spiritual perspective, language must be both **truthful and compassionate**. It must reflect the divine light within the individual, even when describing challenges.

It should never be used to control, categorize, or diminish.

From Labels to Liberation

Labels can serve a purpose when used thoughtfully – particularly for accessing services or clarifying needs. However, many traditional labels limit more than they liberate.

Instead of:

- "Low-functioning" → Say: "Requires high support in daily living"
- "Non-verbal" → Say: "Uses non-speaking communication"
- "Defiant" → Say: "Expresses autonomy or distress"
- "Aggressive" → Say: "Communicating overwhelm or unmet needs"

Every shift in language is a shift in consciousness. The goal is not political correctness – it is **sacred accuracy**.

Speaking With (Not About)

Language that honors the soul is relational, not observational. It is spoken **with** autistic individuals, not just about them. This means:

- Always addressing the person directly, even if others are present

- Using preferred identity language (e.g., "autistic person" vs. "person with autism")
- Asking for and respecting communication preferences
- Reflecting the person's lived experience rather than assuming it

To speak with someone is to affirm their presence. To speak about them in their absence – or as if they are not fully there – is a denial of their agency.

Avoiding the "Fix It" Framework

Many systems, including education and therapy, default to language that frames autism as a problem to be solved. Words like "intervention," "treatment," or "correction" often emerge without reflection.

Instead, spiritual language prioritizes **understanding, support, and connection**. Consider:

- "We're supporting sensory regulation" instead of "treating behavior"
- "Building communication bridges" instead of "fixing deficits"
- "Creating space for expression" instead of "reducing symptoms"

Language should reflect partnership – not pathology.

The Role of Silence and Nonverbal Expression

Not all soul-honoring language is spoken. For many autistic individuals, **gestures, stimming, eye contact (or lack thereof), scripting, art, and silence** are powerful communicative tools. These should not be dismissed or "managed" – they should be interpreted as sacred expressions.

For example:

- Rocking may be self-soothing prayer.

- Repetitive scripting may be a doorway to spiritual resonance.

- Silence may be sacred space, not social avoidance.

To honor the soul, we must honor all languages – not just spoken ones.

Affirming Identity Through Speech

Honoring language is also about affirmation. Simple phrases can become spiritual lifelines. When spoken sincerely, they tell the listener: *You are valuable. You are whole.*

Examples:

- "I respect how you communicate."

- "Your way of seeing the world matters."

- "You are not broken."

- "Thank you for being fully yourself."

Words like these realign environments with **unconditional love**.

Addressing Others With Awareness

Language that honors the soul isn't just for use with autistic individuals – it's also for how we speak to families, professionals, and the broader community. Educate others with compassion, not correction.

Instead of scolding someone for using outdated terms, try:

- "You might find this language more respectful…"
- "Actually, many autistic people prefer…"
- "Here's a different way of saying that, based on what we've learned."

This encourages cultural growth while modeling humility and care.

The Inner Language of Self-Talk

Finally, consider the language autistic individuals may use internally. Are they repeating the words others have used to describe them? "Too much," "difficult," "wrong," "weird"?

We must help rewrite these inner scripts. Offer affirming language generously, and you plant seeds of **sacred self-talk** that may last a lifetime.

Practical Exercise: Your Language Inventory

Time Required: 12–15 minutes

Purpose: To increase self-awareness and alignment in speech.

Instructions:

1. List 5 common phrases you use when talking about or to autistic individuals.

2. For each phrase, reflect: Does this honor autonomy, truth, and dignity?

3. Rewrite any that need more compassion, clarity, or empowerment.

4. Practice using your new phrases aloud. Feel their energy shift.

5. Choose one affirmation to speak regularly: *"I choose words that uplift and reflect the soul."*

_____

_____

_____

_____

_____

Chapter 31: Justice as a Spiritual Imperative

Justice is not only a legal or social concept – it is a **sacred principle**. It is the soul's cry for balance, dignity, and rightful belonging. When injustice occurs, it reverberates at every level: personal, communal, and spiritual. For autistic individuals, whose experiences often include exclusion, misunderstanding, and harm, justice is not optional – it is essential.[1]

To view justice as a spiritual imperative is to understand that inclusion, equity, and protection are not just policies – they are **sacred responsibilities**. Wherever autism is met with judgment, restriction, or invisibility, the spiritual path calls us to respond with courage, compassion, and transformation.

Justice Begins with Dignity

Every human being carries an intrinsic divine spark. Justice begins when that sacred worth is **recognized, affirmed, and defended**. For too long, autistic individuals have been viewed through the lens of deficit, disorder, or deviance – language that strips dignity.

True justice demands a radical shift:

- From control to collaboration
- From exclusion to embodiment

- From protectionism to partnership

In spiritual terms, justice is the act of seeing GOD in one another – and acting accordingly.

The Harm of Spiritual Neglect

Justice also involves recognizing where harm has occurred, even unintentionally. Spiritual neglect is the silent omission of autistic individuals from faith, community, or voice. It looks like:

- Denying access to sacred spaces due to behavior or expression
- Assuming someone is "too disabled" to understand spiritual truths
- Designing programs without consulting those they're meant to serve

When systems are built without autistic input, **they fail to reflect divine wholeness**

Justice Is Active, Not Passive

Spiritual justice requires action. It is not enough to feel compassion; we must **move toward repair**. This includes:

- Reforming educational and care systems that enforce conformity
- Advocating for accessible environments in worship, public policy, and health

- Resisting language or practices that reduce autistic people to stereotypes

Ask in every space: *Is justice present here?* If not, be the one to call it in.

Sacred Disruption

Sometimes, justice requires disruption. This does not mean chaos or violence. It means a **holy refusal** to accept unjust norms.

Examples of sacred disruption:

- Challenging discriminatory language in professional settings

- Supporting autistic self-advocates even when their voices are uncomfortable

- Refusing to participate in systems that force suppression over expression

Injustice thrives in silence. Spirit-led disruption breaks that silence with purpose and clarity.

Justice in Policy and Practice

From a spiritual standpoint, every law or policy is a **moral document**. It reveals what a society values – and whom it deems worthy.

To advocate for spiritually aligned policy:

- Promote inclusive education laws that support neurodiversity
- Demand equitable access to healthcare and communication tools
- Encourage legislators to meet directly with autistic individuals and families
- Advocate for crisis response systems rooted in compassion and consent

Spiritual justice is **systemic justice**. It lives in the details of how people are treated day to day.

Restorative Justice and Healing

Justice is not only punitive. It is **restorative**. When harm has occurred – within families, schools, or institutions – justice calls for repair, not retribution.

Principles of spiritual restoration:

- Naming the harm honestly
- Allowing those harmed to lead the healing process
- Creating new agreements built on respect and awareness
- Practicing forgiveness without bypassing accountability

This form of justice heals the soul as well as the system.

Justice for Families and Caregivers

Justice must extend to caregivers and families, who often carry the emotional and logistical weight of navigating unjust systems. Spiritually speaking, justice means creating **ecosystems of support** that do not isolate, burden, or shame.

Support includes:

- Financial and emotional respite care
- Transparent systems for education, therapy, and transition planning
- Family-inclusive spiritual practices and education
- Recognition and celebration of caregiver strength – not just sacrifice

Where families are supported, justice flourishes.

Justice as a Daily Spiritual Practice

Justice is not a distant goal – it is a daily choice. We practice it every time we:

- Speak up for someone unheard
- Create space for diverse ways of being
- Refuse to look away when a soul is dismissed

These are not just moral acts – they are sacred acts.

A Blessing for Just Action

"May my words protect the vulnerable.

May my presence challenge what is broken.

May my hands rebuild what was harmed.

May my spirit remain committed to sacred justice."

Practical Exercise: A Justice Reflection Map

Time Required: 10–12 minutes

Purpose: To uncover areas where you can bring spiritual justice into action.

Instructions:

1. Draw a large circle on paper. Write "Spiritual Justice" in the center.

2. Around the circle, list 5 areas you influence (home, work, worship, advocacy, caregiving, etc.).

3. For each area, ask:

    - Where might injustice be occurring?
    - Where is dignity being honored or denied?
    - What one change can I make to promote justice here?

4. Commit to one justice-centered action this week. Say aloud: *"Let justice flow through me."*

_____

_____

_____

_____

_____

_____

NOTES:

Chapter 32: Infusing Policy with Purpose

Policy, at its core, is not just a set of rules. It is a **moral framework** that shapes how people are treated, valued, and included. When designed thoughtfully, policy becomes an instrument of justice, dignity, and transformation. When created without soul, it becomes a mechanism of exclusion, control, and harm.[1]

To truly support autistic individuals, policies must reflect more than administrative goals – they must reflect **purpose**. This chapter calls on us to infuse spiritual values into policy-making, ensuring that systems do not just serve efficiently, but **uplift human worth**.

The Soul of Policy

Behind every IEP, healthcare law, housing program, or employment initiative is a question: *Whose needs matter?* Purpose-driven policies arise from a commitment to **sacred inclusion** – where all people, regardless of neurotype, are seen as worthy of access, voice, and safety.

A policy infused with purpose:

- Centers lived experience

- Promotes autonomy over compliance

- Builds ecosystems of care, not control

- Is responsive, not reactive

These are not lofty ideals – they are spiritual imperatives.

Designing With, Not For

Too often, autistic individuals are the subject of policy – but not the authors of it. This reinforces a power imbalance that dehumanizes rather than empowers.

Infusing purpose begins with **participation**:

- Invite autistic voices to co-author policy language

- Offer accessible feedback tools (surveys, AAC-friendly platforms, focus groups)

- Compensate lived-experience consultants equitably

- Honor diverse communication preferences in meetings and hearings

When autistic people shape policy, **policy becomes compassionate and informed**.

The Danger of Compliance-Centered Systems

Many institutional policies – especially in education and healthcare – are built on a **compliance-first mentality**. This rewards obedience and penalizes difference. It often leads to:

- Overuse of restraints or seclusion
- Denial of sensory accommodations
- Suppression of stimming or scripting
- Exclusion from general education settings

Purposeful policy, by contrast, prioritizes **understanding, regulation, and relational safety**. It does not seek to erase difference but to support it with intention and grace.

Language as Policy

Words shape worldviews. Policy that honors autistic individuals must use language that is:

- Clear and inclusive
- Strengths-based rather than deficit-oriented
- Rooted in respect, not pity or fear

Avoiding outdated or offensive terminology in legal documents signals **a cultural shift toward dignity**. Every clause, sentence, and title becomes a vessel for values.

Accessibility Is Spiritual

Accessibility is often framed as a technical requirement. But from a spiritual standpoint, accessibility is an **act of love**. It says: *You belong here. You are welcome as you are.*

Purpose-driven policy ensures:

- Multiple formats for communication and documentation
- Sensory-friendly physical spaces
- Flexibility in scheduling and participation
- Reduced bureaucracy that removes unnecessary stressors

Accessibility should be embedded in all policies – not tacked on as an afterthought.

Funding with Integrity

How resources are distributed reveals a society's soul. Policies that reflect spiritual purpose **direct funding toward care, empowerment, and healing** – not just compliance, surveillance, or containment.

Examples include:

- Prioritizing funding for inclusive classrooms
- Offering grants for AAC devices and sensory supports
- Subsidizing community housing with spiritual and social enrichment options
- Paying support professionals living wages to reduce burnout and turnover

Budgets are spiritual documents. They speak louder than mission statements.

Policy as Protection and Possibility

At their best, policies protect the vulnerable while creating **pathways to thriving**. They are tools of both defense and vision. Purpose-driven policy:

- Guarantees rights to education, healthcare, and housing
- Provides mechanisms for grievance, redress, and accountability
- Fosters cultural change alongside systemic change

Policies must not merely prevent harm – they must **actively promote flourishing**.

Spiritual Oversight and Policy Ethics

Every policy team should include a spiritual advocate –someone who asks:

- Is this policy rooted in dignity?
- Have all voices been heard?
- Who benefits – and who is excluded?
- Are we shaping this from love or fear?

Purpose requires **constant reflection and recalibration**. What begins with good intent must be checked regularly for impact and alignment.

Modeling Sacred Leadership

Those in positions of power – administrators, educators, lawmakers – must lead with **integrity, humility, and accountability**. Purpose-infused leadership:

- Acknowledges when systems have failed
- Invites feedback without defensiveness
- Centers those most affected by decisions
- Acts swiftly when justice demands it

Policy is not static – it is **alive**. It must evolve as our collective consciousness does.

Practical Exercise: Your Personal Policy Audit

Time Required: 15 minutes

Purpose: To reflect on how your own decisions and practices align with purpose-driven values.

Instructions:

1. Choose one "policy" you are part of – a school rule, family decision, workplace protocol.

2. Ask:
   - Who created it? Was it inclusive?
   - Whose needs does it serve? Whose does it ignore?
   - Does it support autonomy, dignity, and growth?

3. Identify one way to adjust or advocate for a change aligned with spiritual purpose.

4. Write a purpose-based mission for this new policy: *"This policy exists to protect, uplift, and include…"*

_____

_____

_____

_____

_____

NOTES:

Chapter 33: Empowering the Spirit of the Advocate

Advocacy is more than activism – it is a **spiritual calling**. It is the voice of the soul rising on behalf of another, the sacred act of standing in love, courage, and truth when systems fall short. For those who advocate on behalf of autistic individuals, the path is often filled with obstacles. But when rooted in spiritual strength, advocacy becomes **transformational** – for both the advocate and those they serve.[1]

This chapter speaks directly to the advocate's spirit: to encourage, fortify, and renew. It offers tools for embodying justice, compassion, and clarity, without burning out or compromising purpose.

The Sacred Role of the Advocate

To advocate is to serve as a bridge – between need and access, silence and voice, margin and inclusion. Advocates often:

- Navigate school systems, healthcare, or legal barriers
- Translate between neurotypical and neurodivergent perspectives
- Hold space for emotions that others may not understand

- Witness injustice and call for systemic change

But most of all, they **affirm worth**. They remind the world that every life matters – and every life deserves support.

Inner Anchors: Advocacy from the Soul

Sustainable advocacy must come from a place of spiritual grounding. External outcomes are never fully in our control – but **inner alignment is**.

Ask regularly:

- What guides my advocacy? Love or anger?
- Am I trying to fix people or uplift them?
- Is this action aligned with the values I hold sacred?

These check-ins ensure that advocacy remains **heart-led, not ego-driven**.

Embodying the Message

The most powerful advocacy doesn't always happen at a podium or policy meeting – it happens in how we live.

We advocate when we:

- Model inclusive behavior
- Speak affirming language
- Educate others with humility and compassion

- Create space for others to speak for themselves

Your energy carries as much weight as your words. Advocacy that honors the soul is **peaceful, powerful, and present**.

Knowing When to Lead – and When to Step Aside

Empowerment means not only speaking **for** others, but ensuring they have the tools and opportunity to speak **for themselves**. This is especially true when advocating for autistic self-advocates.

Ask:

- Is this moment about my voice – or making space for theirs?
- Am I amplifying their message – or replacing it?
- Have I asked them what they want and need from my support?

True empowerment requires **humility and listening**.

Reframing "Hard" Conversations

Advocates often encounter resistance – from institutions, families, or even within themselves. Spiritually grounded advocacy reframes these moments not as walls, but as **sacred invitations**.

Every "no" is an opportunity to:

- Plant seeds for future growth

- Model grace and resilience

- Share truth without shame or aggression

Advocacy done with dignity leaves **a legacy of possibility** – even if the outcome isn't immediate.

Protecting the Advocate's Energy

To give from a depleted spirit is not advocacy – it is martyrdom. Advocates must fiercely protect their own **inner ecosystem**.

Support yourself with:

- Grounding rituals (prayer, breathwork, meditation)

- Restorative breaks away from advocacy work

- Community support with those who uplift and understand

- Emotional release (journaling, movement, counseling)

Burnout serves no one. **A well-nourished advocate is a lasting advocate**.

Advocacy Across Roles

You don't have to be a lawyer or public speaker to be an advocate. Spiritual advocacy is accessible to:

- Parents who choose respectful language

- Teachers who honor sensory needs in the classroom

- Clergy who make worship more inclusive

- Employers who accommodate without judgment
- Neighbors who offer kindness over curiosity

Every act of advocacy is a **ripple of change**.

Advocacy as Prayer

When advocacy is rooted in soul and spirit, it becomes a form of **living prayer**. Your words become affirmations, your actions become offerings, your presence becomes a ministry of love.

Consider affirmations such as:

- "May I speak truth with clarity and compassion."
- "May justice flow through my choices."
- "May I uplift without overpowering."
- "May I be a channel for healing change."

These keep your advocacy connected to purpose, even in moments of fatigue or frustration.

Practical Exercise: The Advocate's Reflection

Time Required: 10–12 minutes

Purpose: To realign your advocacy work with spiritual purpose and clarity.

Instructions:

1. Write down the name of one person you currently advocate for (or have in the past).

2. Reflect: What sacred truth about this person are you trying to defend or uplift?

3. Ask yourself:

    - Is my approach rooted in fear, anger, hope, or love?
    - What does this person most need from me now – presence, power, or protection?
    - Where do I need support or healing in my own advocacy?

4. Create a short blessing or prayer for your continued work. Example:

   "May my voice honor the voiceless. May my heart stay soft but strong. May justice be served through my hands."

_____

_____

_____

Chapter 34: Redefining Safety with Compassion

Safety is often defined by rules, protocols, and control. But in a spiritual sense, safety is much deeper – it is the **felt sense of being seen, respected, and allowed to exist fully**. For autistic individuals, traditional notions of safety can feel like confinement. What institutions call "safe" can feel unsafe to a neurodivergent person when it excludes their sensory needs, autonomy, or authentic expression.[1]

This chapter invites us to **redefine safety** through the lens of compassion. It offers a spiritually aligned model for safety that centers peace, dignity, and co-regulation rather than surveillance or restriction.

What Is True Safety?

True safety is not merely the absence of threat. It is the **presence of trust, comfort, and acceptance**. It allows a person to:

- Be themselves without fear
- Express needs without punishment
- Regulate emotions without shame

- Navigate space without hypervigilance

In spiritual terms, safety is an atmosphere of grace. It is a **sanctuary of soul-level welcome**.

The Problem with Control-Based Safety

Many institutions still operate on a "control equals safety" model. This leads to:

- Overuse of restraints or seclusion
- Overreliance on compliance-based behavior plans
- Removal from classroom or community settings during distress
- Ignoring the sensory and emotional needs of the individual

While these measures may reduce disruption, they **do not create real safety**. They may calm the environment while traumatizing the person.

Compassion as the Foundation of Safety

Compassion sees beyond the behavior to the **underlying need**. It asks:

- What pain, confusion, or overwhelm is this person experiencing?

- How can I respond in a way that affirms rather than corrects?
- What kind of environment would soothe this soul?

From a spiritual perspective, compassion is the beginning of all safety. It calms the nervous system, builds trust, and allows the heart to open.

Sensory Safety: A Sacred Right

Many autistic individuals live in a world that constantly overwhelms their senses. Bright lights, loud noises, crowded rooms, and rigid routines can trigger distress.

A compassion-centered safety plan includes:

- Quiet zones and sensory retreat spaces
- Flexible lighting and noise control
- Access to tools like fidgets, weighted items, or ear defenders
- Understanding when stimming is a form of self-protection

These are not luxuries – they are **sacred accommodations**.

Relational Safety

Safety is not just physical – it is relational. A spiritually safe environment is one where people:

- Are greeted with warmth and openness

- Are listened to deeply, even when they don't use words
- Are allowed to set boundaries
- Are not punished for emotional expression

In spiritual terms, every relationship is an altar. We are called to approach one another with **reverence**.

Co-Regulation as a Spiritual Practice

When a person is overwhelmed, they often need another person to help them regulate. This is called **co-regulation** – and it is one of the most sacred offerings we can give.

Co-regulation means:

- Staying calm and grounded in the presence of distress
- Offering soothing words, tones, or silence
- Being a steady presence without trying to fix or rush

It says: *You are not alone in this moment. I am with you.* That, more than any rule, creates true safety.

Safety Plans Rooted in Voice

Too often, "safety plans" are made **for** autistic individuals without their input. These plans may focus on behavior modification rather than emotional or sensory support.

A compassion-based safety plan:

- Includes the individual in its creation
- Focuses on what helps them feel calm, secure, and respected
- Lists strategies for prevention – not just response
- Uses respectful, strengths-based language

Let the person define their own safe space. It is **a spiritual right to be the author of one's own peace**.

Crisis Response with Dignity

In times of distress or meltdown, safety must still include dignity. This means:

- Avoiding isolation, physical restraint, or threats
- Remaining emotionally available and calm
- Allowing expression to move through rather than be shut down
- Focusing on recovery, not punishment

Dignity-centered crisis response transforms chaos into **a moment of healing**.

A Spiritual Safety Statement

Consider affirming this spiritual safety principle in your space:

"Here, safety means more than control.

It means presence, permission, and peace.

All are welcome in their fullness.

Compassion is our first response.

Dignity is never negotiable."

Let this be the heart of all policies, practices, and interactions.

Practical Exercise: Your Sacred Safety Scan

Time Required: 10–12 minutes

Purpose: To reflect on whether your environments offer true, compassionate safety.

Instructions:

1. Choose one environment you influence (home, classroom, clinic, spiritual center).

2. Ask:

   - Is this space welcoming to neuro-diverse sensory needs?
   - Are emotional expressions met with support or suppression?
   - Do individuals have autonomy and input?
   - Are safety measures rooted in trust – or control?

3. Identify 1–2 compassionate changes you can make this week.

4. Post or write your own version of a spiritual safety statement for that space.

_____

_____

_____

_____

NOTES:

Chapter 35: Building Conscious Communities

A conscious community is not just one that includes autistic individuals – it is one that **recognizes, values, and is transformed by them**. It is a community where all neurotypes are seen as sacred expressions of humanity, and where diversity is woven into the spiritual and social fabric.

In a world still healing from the divisions of ignorance and fear, building conscious communities is not optional – it is a spiritual mandate.[1] This chapter explores how we can create environments that go beyond access and embrace **interdependence, authenticity, and soul-aligned belonging**.

What Is a Conscious Community?

A conscious community is intentional. It is a space – physical or virtual – that centers:

- Presence over productivity
- Relationship over regulation
- Voice over silence
- Spirit over structure

In such communities, people are not asked to fit in; they are welcomed to **fully show up** as themselves. Conscious communities are built with the understanding that every soul contributes wisdom – and every person matters.

Inclusion as a Spiritual Practice

Inclusion in a conscious community is not about allowing someone to join what already exists – it is about co-creating a new way of being together. This inclusion is spiritual because it is based in:

- Deep listening
- Nonjudgmental presence
- Shared vulnerability
- Commitment to mutual growth

True inclusion asks: *How can we evolve together through the presence of each person?* This question reorients communities from tolerance to **transformation**.

Designing With Autistic Voices

To build a conscious community that honors neurodiversity, autistic individuals must be **co-creators, not just participants**.

Conscious communities:

- Include autistic individuals in planning, leadership, and evaluation

- Use accessible and multimodal communication strategies
- Hold space for nonverbal and nontraditional expressions
- Design physical spaces with sensory awareness

A community built **with** rather than **for** becomes a spiritual classroom for compassion, creativity, and connection.

Rethinking Space and Time

Traditional communities are often built on norms that alienate neurodivergent individuals – tight schedules, overstimulating spaces, and rigid social expectations.

Conscious communities rethink:

- Space: Provide quiet zones, natural light, sensory-friendly areas
- Time: Allow for pacing, processing, and flexible participation
- Flow: Reduce transitions, offer visual cues, and create ritual for grounding

These shifts honor the sacred rhythm each person carries.

Shared Rituals and Collective Spirit

Rituals anchor communities. In conscious communities, rituals are:

- Centered on connection rather than control

- Inclusive of diverse communication and expression
- Designed to affirm worth and invite presence

Examples:

- Group gratitude circles where all contributions are valid
- Opening meditations or breathwork for co-regulation
- Art, music, or nature-based expression as shared spiritual practice

These rituals elevate community into **communion**.

Mutuality Over Hierarchy

Traditional community models often rely on top-down leadership. Conscious communities operate through **mutuality**, where power is shared and leadership rotates or flows naturally.

This looks like:

- Peer-led support groups
- Co-facilitated events with autistic and neurotypical leaders
- Feedback loops where all members shape direction and vision

Power in conscious communities is not something to **hold** – it is something to **flow** through, with humility and trust.

Conflict as Sacred Conversation

Conflict is not the enemy of community – it is an opportunity for **deeper authenticity**. Conscious communities hold space for discomfort without reactivity.

Conflict transformation tools include:

- Nonviolent communication
- Restorative circles
- Acknowledgment of harm with accountability, not shame
- Community agreements created by all members

These tools allow community members to grow **through each other**, not away from each other.

Sustaining the Community Spirit

To stay conscious, a community must:

- Reflect regularly: What's working? Who's missing?
- Recommit to core values and update agreements as needed
- Protect against burnout through shared responsibility
- Celebrate growth and milestones with joy

A spiritually aligned community is **alive**. It breathes, stretches, and transforms with the people who shape it.

Beyond the Local: Creating Networks of Consciousness

While conscious communities often begin locally, their ripple can extend globally. Online platforms, advocacy groups, and sacred networks can link communities across distance – spreading light, resources, and solidarity.

Consider:

- Hosting virtual circles for spiritual neurodiversity
- Sharing models of conscious community formation
- Partnering with schools, clinics, and faith spaces to expand inclusion

The more we model conscious community, the more we invite a **collective awakening**.

Practical Exercise: Community Vision Mandala

Time Required: 10–15 minutes

Purpose: To visualize and commit to your role in creating or deepening a conscious community.

Instructions:

1. Draw a large circle on a page—this represents your ideal conscious community.

2. Inside the circle, write or sketch:

    - Core values (e.g., listening, belonging, respect)
    - Practices or rituals you want to see
    - People or groups you'd like to include
    - How autistic individuals will help shape this space

3. Outside the circle, list action steps to begin creating or enhancing this community (e.g., reach out, host a gathering, share ideas).

4. Place the mandala somewhere visible as a spiritual reminder and intention.

_____

_____

_____

_____

_____

NOTES:

Chapter 36: Affirming Sacred Purpose

To walk this Earth is to walk with purpose. For every human being – autistic or not – there exists a divine intention. Yet for too long, the narrative surrounding autism has focused on deficit, disorder, and delay, rather than on **destiny, design, and depth**.

This chapter seeks to restore what has always been true: every autistic soul carries a **sacred purpose**. That purpose may not always align with societal norms or timelines, but it is no less holy. Whether it shows up in a passion for patterns, a depth of presence, or a sensitivity to spirit, purpose pulses through the autistic experience.

To affirm sacred purpose is to reclaim the **spiritual wholeness** of every life.

What Is Sacred Purpose?

Sacred purpose is not about employment, education, or social success – though it may include those. It is the **soul's mission**, the energy and essence an individual brings into the world, simply by being who they are.

Sacred purpose may express itself through:

- A gift for sensing emotions
- A drive to organize or systematize
- A powerful capacity for solitude and stillness
- A deep relationship with music, animals, or nature
- A fierce devotion to justice and truth

When we shift our lens from function to **fulfillment**, we begin to witness purpose in every moment.

The Danger of Conditional Worth

Society often assigns worth based on productivity, independence, or conformity. But sacred purpose is not earned – it is **intrinsic**.

This means:

- A non-speaking person is just as purposeful as a public speaker
- A child who loves lining up objects is expressing as much soul as one reciting scripture
- A young adult in supported housing is no less sacred than one attending college

The minute we tie worth to output, we disconnect from divine reality[1]. Purpose does not wait for milestones. It is always active, even when unseen.

Recognizing Purpose in the Present

Spiritual advocacy calls us to notice and name the sacred in ordinary moments. A parent might say:

- "When you line up those toys, I see your eye for symmetry."
- "Your love for numbers reminds me of the order of the universe."
- "You don't talk, but your energy teaches me how to listen."

These affirmations **anchor identity** in something deeper than diagnosis. They allow autistic individuals to experience themselves as meaningful, not just manageable.

Walking With Purpose as a Family or Team

When families and support professionals recognize sacred purpose, their entire approach shifts:

- Instead of "What will they become?" they ask, "Who are they already?"
- Instead of measuring progress against norms, they celebrate presence and growth

- Instead of fearing the future, they partner with it

This posture builds environments of **spiritual trust and patience**.

Supporting Purpose Without Pressure

To affirm purpose is not to rush or force it. Sacred purpose unfolds at the soul's pace.

Support may look like:

- Exposing the individual to a wide variety of experiences without expectation
- Watching for signs of joy, focus, or curiosity
- Offering tools to explore their interests (e.g., art supplies, instruments, nature walks)
- Being willing to sit in the unknown, trusting something beautiful is emerging

Purpose cannot be assigned – it must be **revealed and received**.

Lifelong Purpose: Beyond Childhood

Many systems are built around children – but sacred purpose **does not expire at age 18**. Adults with autism continue to evolve, contribute, and grow. Their purpose may include:

- Becoming spiritual teachers through lived example

- Offering wisdom through written or visual expression
- Participating in community in their own rhythm
- Simply holding a frequency of presence that reminds others to slow down and feel

Affirming purpose across the lifespan honors the **eternity of the soul**.

Affirming Our Own Sacred Purpose as Allies

Those who support autistic individuals must also affirm their own purpose – not as saviors, but as **servants of divine unfolding**.

Ask:

- What is my purpose in this relationship?
- How am I being transformed by this person's presence?
- How do I embody dignity, patience, and reverence?

When we align with sacred service, we become partners in healing – not just helpers[2].

Purpose as a Portal to Belonging

When people feel purposeful, they also feel **they belong**. They no longer see themselves as broken, but as **builders of something eternal**. This inner knowing creates ripple effects of confidence, calm, and connection.

To affirm someone's sacred purpose is to say:

- "You are not here by accident. You matter now – not later. Your life is already enough."

Such a message is a balm to every soul – especially one that has been misunderstood.

Practical Exercise: Sacred Purpose Letter

Time Required: 10–15 minutes

Purpose: To affirm sacred purpose in someone you support – and in yourself.

Instructions:

1. Choose an autistic individual you support or love.

2. Write a letter to them (even if they won't read it directly). Include:

    - What makes them unique?
    - What you've learned from their way of being?
    - How you see sacred purpose in them right now – not in the future?

3. Now, write a short paragraph to yourself:

    - What is your sacred role in this relationship?
    - What purpose is being revealed through your journey together?

4. Reflect on how this awareness can shape your daily interactions.

_____

_____

_____

_____

NOTES:

Conclusion: Embracing the Sacred Path Forward

Autism is not a puzzle to be solved. It is a path to be honored.

As we come to the close of this book, may you pause and reflect – not only on what you've read but on who you are becoming. Whether you are a parent seeking peace, a professional striving to serve with greater soul, or an advocate lifting voices that deserve to be heard, you are part of something sacred. You are part of a movement not just for awareness or acceptance, but for awakening.

We have explored autism not as a deficit or limitation, but as a sacred expression of humanity – complete, complex, and deeply spiritual. In doing so, we have redefined what it means to love, to serve, to listen, and to lead.

Throughout this journey, you have learned tools. But more importantly, you've reclaimed truths:

- That autistic individuals are not broken – they are brilliant in ways often unseen.

- That presence and patience are more powerful than pressure.

- That dignity begins with seeing the soul before the diagnosis.

- That every behavior is communication and every moment is an opportunity to honor sacred design.

In choosing to walk this path with reverence, you become a witness to transformation – not just in those you support, but in yourself.

This is not the end. It is a threshold.

The real work begins as you return to your family, your classroom, your clinic, your community –with new eyes and an open heart. You carry with you now a deeper sensitivity, a spiritual compass, and a reminder that every human being, regardless of neurology, is here for a reason.

May you speak with compassion.

May you serve with humility.

May you honor the quiet miracles unfolding in each life you touch.

You were not drawn to this book by accident. Your presence in this movement matters. Your care is part of the healing the world needs.

Together, let us build a world where neurodiversity is not only respected but revered – where autistic individuals are not just included but deeply cherished for who they are and what they bring.

Let us no longer ask, "How can we fix them?" but instead, "What can we learn from them?"

Let us no longer strive for normalcy, but for sacred connection.

Let us go forward in love, in purpose, and in peace.

Thank you for walking this journey.

Thank you for choosing to see differently.

Thank you for choosing to love more deeply.

May the light within you continue to shine, and may you always see the divine light shining in others.

And so it is.

Amen.

_____

_____

_____

_____

_____

_____

_____

_____

_____

NOTES:

Footnotes

SECTION ONE: For Parents of Autistic Individuals

Chapter 1: Seeing the Divine in Your Child

[1] Blanchard, A. (2020). *Reframing Autism: From Deficit to Difference.* Spectrum Spirit Press.

[2] Siegel, D. J., & Bryson, T. P. (2016). *The Whole-Brain Child.* Random House.

[3] Narvaez, D. (2018). *Neurodiversity and Indigenous Wisdom.* Journal of Human Development.

[4] Montessori, M. (1966). *The Secret of Childhood.* Ballantine Books.

[5] Goleman, D. (1995). *Emotional Intelligence.* Bantam.

Chapter 2: Parenting with Presence

[1] Greenspan, S. I., & Wieder, S. (2006). ENGAGING AUTISM. Da Capo Press.

[2] Siegel, D. J. (2010). THE MINDFUL THERAPIST. W. W. Norton & Company.

[3] Tolle, E. (1999). THE POWER OF NOW. New World Library.

[4] Delahooke, M. (2019). BEYOND BEHAVIORS. PESI Publishing.

[5] Neff, K. (2011). SELF-COMPASSION: THE PROVEN POWER OF BEING KIND TO YOURSELF. William Morrow.

Chapter 3: Spiritual Approaches to Sensory Sensitivities

[1] Bogdashina, O. (2016). SENSORY PERCEPTUAL ISSUES IN AUTISM AND ASPERGER SYNDROME. Jessica Kingsley Publishers.

[2] Chopra, D. (2004). THE BOOK OF SECRETS: UNLOCKING THE HIDDEN DIMENSIONS OF YOUR LIFE. Harmony.

[3] Delahooke, M. (2019). BEYOND BEHAVIORS. PESI Publishing.

[4] Grandin, T. (2006). THINKING IN PICTURES. Vintage Books.

[5] Siegel, D. J., & Bryson, T. P. (2020). THE POWER OF SHOWING UP. Ballantine Books.

Chapter 4: Trusting Their Path

[1] Neufeld, G., & Maté, G. (2004). HOLD ON TO YOUR KIDS. Ballantine Books.

[2] Delahooke, M. (2019). BEYOND BEHAVIORS. PESI Publishing.

[3] Walsch, N. D. (1999). CONVERSATIONS WITH GOD FOR PARENTS. Hampton Roads.

[4] Tsabary, S. (2016). THE AWAKENED FAMILY. TarcherPerigee.

Chapter 5: Creating a Sacred Home Environment

[1] Grandin, T. (2013). THE AUTISTIC BRAIN. Houghton Mifflin Harcourt.

[2] Siegel, D. J., & Bryson, T. P. (2016). THE WHOLE-BRAIN CHILD. Random House.

[3] Bogdashina, O. (2016). SENSORY PERCEPTUAL ISSUES IN AUTISM AND ASPERGER SYNDROME. Jessica Kingsley.

[4] Kranowitz, C. S. (2005). THE OUT-OF-SYNC CHILD. Penguin.

[5] Ayres, A. J. (2005). SENSORY INTEGRATION AND THE CHILD. Western Psychological Services.

[6] Healy, J. M. (1998). FAILURE TO CONNECT: HOW COMPUTERS AFFECT OUR CHILDREN'S MINDS. Simon & Schuster.

Chapter 6: Heart-to-Heart Communication

[1] Siegel, D. J. (2010). THE WHOLE-BRAIN CHILD: 12 REVOLUTIONARY STRATEGIES TO NURTURE YOUR CHILD'S DEVELOPING MIND. Bantam Books.

[2] Greenspan, S. I., & Wieder, S. (1998). THE CHILD WITH SPECIAL NEEDS: ENCOURAGING INTELLECTUAL AND EMOTIONAL GROWTH. Da Capo Press.

[3] Myles, B. S., & Southwick, J. (2005). ASPERGER SYNDROME AND DIFFICULT MOMENTS. Autism Asperger Publishing Company.

[4] Prizant, B. M. (2015). UNIQUELY HUMAN: A DIFFERENT WAY OF SEEING AUTISM. Simon & Schuster.

Chapter 7: Faith, Hope, and Emotional Strength

[1]Neff, K. (2011). SELF-COMPASSION: THE PROVEN POWER OF BEING KIND TO YOURSELF. William Morrow.

[2]Van Der Kolk, B. (2014). THE BODY KEEPS THE SCORE: BRAIN, MIND, AND BODY IN THE HEALING OF TRAUMA. Viking.

[3]Tsabary, S. (2010). THE CONSCIOUS PARENT: TRANSFORMING OURSELVES, EMPOWERING OUR CHILDREN. Namaste Publishing.

[4]Brown, B. (2015). RISING STRONG: HOW THE ABILITY TO RESET TRANSFORMS THE WAY WE LIVE, LOVE, PARENT, AND LEAD. Spiegel & Grau.

Chapter 8: Navigating the System with Grace

[1]Nhat Hanh, T. (2002). CREATING TRUE PEACE: ENDING VIOLENCE IN YOURSELF, YOUR FAMILY, YOUR COMMUNITY, AND THE WORLD. Free Press.

[2]Kabat-Zinn, J. (2013). FULL CATASTROPHE LIVING: USING THE WISDOM OF YOUR BODY AND MIND TO FACE STRESS, PAIN, AND ILLNESS. Bantam.

[3]Greene, R. W., & Ablon, J. S. (2006). TREATING EXPLOSIVE KIDS: THE COLLABORATIVE PROBLEM-SOLVING APPROACH. Guilford Press.

[4]Wright, P. D., & Wright, P. D. (2006). WRIGHTSLAW: FROM EMOTIONS TO ADVOCACY – THE SPECIAL EDUCATION SURVIVAL GUIDE. Harbor House Law Press.

Chapter 9: Celebrating Progress with Gratitude

[1]Emmons, R. A., & McCullough, M. E. (2003). *Counting Blessings Versus Burdens: An Experimental Investigation of Gratitude and Subjective Well-Being in Daily Life*. Journal of Personality and Social Psychology, 84(2), 377–389.

[2]Siegel, D. J., & Bryson, T. P. (2020). *The Power of Showing Up: How Parental Presence Shapes Who Our Kids Become and How Their Brains Get Wired*. Ballantine Books.

[3]Kushner, H. S. (1981). *When Bad Things Happen to Good People*. Schocken Books.

Chapter 10: Siblings and Soul Lessons

[1]Hartley, S. L., & Sikora, D. M. (2009). SIBLING RELATIONSHIPS OF CHILDREN WITH AUTISM: CHARACTERISTICS AND INTERVENTION APPROACHES. Journal of Intellectual & Developmental Disability, 34(1), 17–27.

[2]Meyer, D. J., & Vadasy, P. F. (2008). LIVING WITH A BROTHER OR SISTER WITH SPECIAL NEEDS: A BOOK FOR SIBS. University of Washington Press.

[3]Chopra, D. (1997). THE SEVEN SPIRITUAL LAWS FOR PARENTS: GUIDING YOUR CHILDREN TO SUCCESS AND FULFILLMENT. Harmony Books.

[4]Glasberg, B. A. (2000). BROTHERS, SISTERS, AND AUTISM: A PARENT'S GUIDE TO SUPPORTING SIBLINGS. Woodbine House.

Chapter 11: Planning with Peace of Mind

[1]Wright, S. (2013). SPECIAL NEEDS TRUSTS: PROTECT YOUR CHILD'S FINANCIAL FUTURE. Nolo Press.

[2]Kubler-Ross, E., & Kessler, D. (2004). ON GRIEF AND GRIEVING: FINDING THE MEANING OF GRIEF THROUGH THE FIVE STAGES OF LOSS. Scribner.

Chapter 12: You Were Chosen for This Journey

[1]Siegel, D. J., & Hartzell, M. (2013). *Parenting from the Inside Out: How a Deeper Self-Understanding Can Help You Raise Children Who Thrive.* TarcherPerigee.

[2]Williamson, M. (1994). *A Return to Love: Reflections on the Principles of A Course in Miracles.* HarperOne.

[3]Walsch, N. D. (1995). *Conversations with God: An Uncommon Dialogue, Book 1.* Putnam.

SECTION TWO: For Support Professionals

Chapter 13: Seeing the Individual Beyond the Label

[1]Prizant, B. M. (2015). *Uniquely Human: A Different Way of Seeing Autism.* Simon & Schuster.

[2]Ne'eman, A. (2010). *Loud Hands: Autistic People, Speaking.* The Autistic Press.

Chapter 14: Creating Sensory and Spirit Friendly Spaces

[1]Grandin, T. (2013). THE AUTISTIC BRAIN: THINKING ACROSS THE SPECTRUM. Houghton Mifflin Harcourt.

[2]Koenig, H. G. (2008). MEDICINE, RELIGION, AND HEALTH: WHERE SCIENCE AND SPIRITUALITY MEET. Templeton Foundation Press.

Chapter 15: Holistic Communications Tools

[1] Light, J., & McNaughton, D. (2012). *Supporting the Communication, Language, and Literacy Development of Children with Complex Communication Needs*. Paul H. Brookes Publishing Co.

Chapter 16: Being Trauma-Informed and Spiritually-Aware

[1]Kapp, S. K. (2020). AUTISTIC COMMUNITY AND THE NEURODIVERSITY MOVEMENT: STORIES FROM THE FRONTLINE. Palgrave Macmillan.

[2]van der Kolk, B. (2015). THE BODY KEEPS THE SCORE: BRAIN, MIND, AND BODY IN THE HEALING OF TRAUMA. Penguin Books.

Chapter 17: Recognizing Spiritual Intelligence

[1]Gardner, H. (2000). *Intelligence Reframed: Multiple Intelligences for the 21st Century*. Basic Books.

[2]Zohar, D., & Marshall, I. (2000). *SQ: Connecting with Our Spiritual Intelligence*. Bloomsbury Publishing.

Chapter 18: Serving the Family as a Whole

[1]Turnbull, A., Turnbull, R., Erwin, E. J., Soodak, L. C., & Shogren, K. A. (2015). FAMILIES, PROFESSIONALS, AND EXCEPTIONALITY: POSITIVE OUTCOMES THROUGH PARTNERSHIPS AND TRUST. Pearson.

[2]Siegel, D. J., & Bryson, T. P. (2011). THE WHOLE-BRAIN CHILD: 12 REVOLUTIONARY STRATEGIES TO NURTURE YOUR CHILD'S DEVELOPING MIND. Bantam.

Chapter 19: Guiding with Meaning and Purpose

[1]Shea, V. (2018). POSITIVE BEHAVIOR SUPPORT: STRATEGIES FOR TEACHERS AND PROFESSIONALS. Routledge.

[2]Hagner, D. & Cooney, B. F. (2005). SELF-DETERMINATION AND CHOICE: MAKING A POSITIVE DIFFERENCE IN PEOPLE'S LIVES. Brookes Publishing.

Chapter 20: Sacred Structure and Routines

[1] Koenig, K. P., & Rudney, S. G. (2010). *Performance Challenges for Children and Youth with Sensory Processing Disorders: A Survey of Parents and Teachers*. American Journal of Occupational Therapy.

[2] Dunn, W. (2007). *Supporting Children to Participate Successfully in Everyday Life by Using Sensory Processing Knowledge*. Infants & Young Children.

Chapter 21: Mindfulness and Grounding Practices

[1] Kabat-Zinn, J. (2013). FULL CATASTROPHE LIVING: USING THE WISDOM OF YOUR BODY AND MIND TO FACE STRESS, PAIN, AND ILLNESS. Bantam Books.

[2] Bogdashina, O. (2016). SENSORY PERCEPTUAL ISSUES IN AUTISM AND ASPERGER SYNDROME: DIFFERENT SENSORY EXPERIENCES - DIFFERENT PERCEPTUAL WORLDS. Jessica Kingsley Publishers.

Chapter 22: Developing Sacred Rapport

[1] Rogers, C. R. (1961). ON BECOMING A PERSON: A THERAPIST'S VIEW OF PSYCHOTHERAPY. Houghton Mifflin Harcourt.

Chapter 23: Ethical Empowerment

[1] Neumeier, S. (2020). AUTISTIC COMMUNITY AND THE NEURODIVERSITY MOVEMENT. Springer.

[2] Bascom, J. (2012). LOUD HANDS: AUTISTIC PEOPLE, SPEAKING. Autistic Self Advocacy Network.

[3] Kapp, S. (2019). AUTISM AND THE SOCIAL MODEL. Palgrave Macmillan.

Chapter 24: Caring for the Whole Beuing

[1] Prizant, B. (2015). UNIQUELY HUMAN: A DIFFERENT WAY OF SEEING AUTISM. Simon & Schuster.

[2] Siegel, D. J. & Bryson, T. P. (2011). THE WHOLE-BRAIN CHILD. Delacorte Press.

SECTION THREE: For Autism Advocates

Chapter 25: The Spiritual Power of Neurodiversity

[1] Kapp, S. (2020). AUTISTIC COMMUNITY AND THE NEURODIVERSITY MOVEMENT. Springer.

[2] Silberman, S. (2015). NEUROTRIBES: THE LEGACY OF AUTISM AND THE FUTURE OF NEURODIVERSITY. Avery Publishing.

Chapter 26: Centering Autistic Voices

[1] Bascom, J. (2012). LOUD HANDS: AUTISTIC PEOPLE, SPEAKING. Autistic Self Advocacy Network.

[2] Biklen, D. (2005). AUTISM AND THE MYTH OF THE PERSON ALONE. NYU Press.

Chapter 27: Dignity for All

[1] Kim, E. (2016). CURATING ACCESS: DISABILITY ART ACTIVISM AND THE POLITICS OF DIGNITY. Duke University Press.

Chapter 28: Creating Sacred Inclusion

[1] Ault, M. (2010). INCLUSIVE SPIRITUALITY: EMBRACING NEURODIVERSE WORSHIP. Harmony Press.

Chapter 29: Educating with Love and Light

[1] Palmer, P. J. (1998). THE COURAGE TO TEACH: EXPLORING THE INNER LANDSCAPE OF A TEACHER'S LIFE. Jossey-Bass.

Chapter 30: Language That Honors the Soul

[1] Biklen, D. (2005). AUTISM AND THE MYTH OF THE PERSON ALONE. NYU Press.

Chapter 31: Justice as Spiritual Imperative

[1] Hooks, Bell. (2000). ALL ABOUT LOVE: NEW VISIONS. William Morrow.

Chapter 32: Infusing Policy with Purpose

[1] Taylor, S. J. (2010). AUTISM AND THE ETHICS OF INCLUSION. Disability Studies Quarterly.

Chapter 33: Empowering the Spirit of the Advocate

[1] Lorde, Audre. (1984). SISTER OUTSIDER: ESSAYS AND SPEECHES. Crossing Press.

Chapter 34: Redefining Safety with Compassion

[1] Prizant, Barry M. (2015). UNIQUELY HUMAN: A DIFFERENT WAY OF SEEING AUTISM. Simon & Schuster.

Chapter 35: Building Conscious Communities

[1] Wheatley, Margaret J. (2002). TURNING TO ONE ANOTHER: SIMPLE CONVERSATIONS TO RESTORE HOPE TO THE FUTURE. Berrett-Koehler Publishers.

Chapter 36: Affirming Sacred Purpose

[1] Palmer, Parker J. (2000). LET YOUR LIFE SPEAK: LISTENING FOR THE VOICE OF VOCATION. Jossey-Bass.

[2] Vanier, Jean. (1998). BECOMING HUMAN. Paulist Press.

Bibliography

SECTION ONE: For Parents of Autistic Individuals

Chapter 1: Seeing the Divine in Your Child

- Blanchard, A. (2020). REFRAMING AUTISM: FROM DEFICIT TO DIFFERENCE. Spectrum Spirit Press.
- Goleman, D. (1995). EMOTIONAL INTELLIGENCE. Bantam.
- Montessori, M. (1966). THE SECRET OF CHILDHOOD. Ballantine Books.
- Narvaez, D. (2018). NEURODIVERSITY AND INDIGENOUS WISDOM. Journal of Human Development.
- Siegel, D. J., & Bryson, T. P. (2016). THE WHOLE-BRAIN CHILD. Random House.

Chapter 2: Chapter 2: Parenting with Presence

- Delahooke, M. (2019). BEYOND BEHAVIORS. PESI Publishing.
- Greenspan, S. I., & Wieder, S. (2006). ENGAGING AUTISM. Da Capo Press.
- Neff, K. (2011). SELF-COMPASSION: THE PROVEN POWER OF BEING KIND TO YOURSELF. William Morrow.
- Siegel, D. J. (2010). THE MINDFUL THERAPIST. W. W. Norton & Company.
- Tolle, E. (1999). THE POWER OF NOW. New World Library.

Chapter 3: Spiritual Approaches to Sensory Sensitives

- Bogdashina, O. (2016). SENSORY PERCEPTUAL ISSUES IN AUTISM AND ASPERGER SYNDROME. Jessica Kingsley Publishers.
- Chopra, D. (2004). THE BOOK OF SECRETS: UNLOCKING THE HIDDEN DIMENSIONS OF YOUR LIFE. Harmony.
- Delahooke, M. (2019). BEYOND BEHAVIORS. PESI Publishing.
- Grandin, T. (2006). THINKING IN PICTURES. Vintage Books.
- Siegel, D. J., & Bryson, T. P. (2020). THE POWER OF SHOWING UP. Ballantine Books.

Chapter 4: Trusting Their Path

- Delahooke, M. (2019). BEYOND BEHAVIORS. PESI Publishing.

- Neufeld, G., & Maté, G. (2004). HOLD ON TO YOUR KIDS. Ballantine Books.

- Tsabary, S. (2016). THE AWAKENED FAMILY. TarcherPerigee.

- Walsch, N. D. (1999). CONVERSATIONS WITH GOD FOR PARENTS. Hampton Roads.

Chapter 5: Creating a Sacred Home Environment

- Ayres, A. J. (2005). SENSORY INTEGRATION AND THE CHILD. Western Psychological Services.

- Bogdashina, O. (2016). SENSORY PERCEPTUAL ISSUES IN AUTISM AND ASPERGER SYNDROME. Jessica Kingsley.

- Grandin, T. (2013). THE AUTISTIC BRAIN. Houghton Mifflin Harcourt.

- Healy, J. M. (1998). FAILURE TO CONNECT. Simon & Schuster.

- Kranowitz, C. S. (2005). THE OUT-OF-SYNC CHILD. Penguin.

- Siegel, D. J., & Bryson, T. P. (2016). THE WHOLE-BRAIN CHILD. Random House.

Chapter 6: Heart-to-Heart Communication

- Greenspan, S. I., & Wieder, S. (1998). *The Child with Special Needs: Encouraging Intellectual and Emotional Growth*. Da Capo Press.

- Myles, B. S., & Southwick, J. (2005). *Asperger Syndrome and Difficult Moments.* Autism Asperger Publishing Company.

- Prizant, B. M. (2015). *Uniquely Human: A Different Way of Seeing Autism.* Simon & Schuster.

- Siegel, D. J. (2010). *The Whole-Brain Child: 12 Revolutionary Strategies to Nurture Your Child's Developing Mind*. Bantam Books.

Chapter 7: Faith, Hope, and Emotional Strength

- Brown, B. (2015). RISING STRONG: HOW THE ABILITY TO RESET TRANSFORMS THE WAY WE LIVE, LOVE, PARENT, AND LEAD. Spiegel & Grau.

- Neff, K. (2011). SELF-COMPASSION: THE PROVEN POWER OF BEING KIND TO YOURSELF. William Morrow.

- Tsabary, S. (2010). THE CONSCIOUS PARENT: TRANSFORMING OURSELVES, EMPOWERING OUR CHILDREN. Namaste Publishing.

- Van Der Kolk, B. (2014). THE BODY KEEPS THE SCORE: BRAIN, MIND, AND BODY IN THE HEALING OF TRAUMA. Viking.

Chapter 8: Navigating the System with Grace

- Greene, R. W., & Ablon, J. S. (2006). TREATING EXPLOSIVE KIDS: THE COLLABORATIVE PROBLEM-SOLVING APPROACH. Guilford Press.

- Kabat-Zinn, J. (2013). FULL CATASTROPHE LIVING: USING THE WISDOM OF YOUR BODY AND MIND TO FACE STRESS, PAIN, AND ILLNESS. Bantam.

- Nhat Hanh, T. (2002). CREATING TRUE PEACE: ENDING VIOLENCE IN YOURSELF, YOUR FAMILY, YOUR COMMUNITY, AND THE WORLD. Free Press.

- Wright, P. D., & Wright, P. D. (2006). WRIGHTSLAW: FROM EMOTIONS TO ADVOCACY – THE SPECIAL EDUCATION SURVIVAL GUIDE. Harbor House Law Press.

Chapter 9: Celebrating Progress with Gratitude

- Emmons, R. A., & McCullough, M. E. (2003). COUNTING BLESSINGS VERSUS BURDENS: AN EXPERIMENTAL INVESTIGATION OF GRATITUDE AND SUBJECTIVE WELL-BEING IN DAILY LIFE. JOURNAL OF PERSONALITY AND SOCIAL PSYCHOLOGY, 84(2), 377–389.

- Kushner, H. S. (1981). WHEN BAD THINGS HAPPEN TO GOOD PEOPLE. Schocken Books.

- Siegel, D. J., & Bryson, T. P. (2020). THE POWER OF SHOWING UP: HOW PARENTAL PRESENCE SHAPES WHO OUR KIDS BECOME AND HOW THEIR BRAINS GET WIRED. Ballantine Books.

Chapter 10: Siblings and Soul Lessons

- Chopra, D. (1997). THE SEVEN SPIRITUAL LAWS FOR PARENTS: GUIDING YOUR CHILDREN TO SUCCESS AND FULFILLMENT. Harmony Books.

- Glasberg, B. A. (2000). BROTHERS, SISTERS, AND AUTISM: A PARENT'S GUIDE TO SUPPORTING SIBLINGS. Woodbine House.

- Hartley, S. L., & Sikora, D. M. (2009). SIBLING RELATIONSHIPS OF CHILDREN WITH AUTISM: CHARACTERISTICS AND INTERVENTION APPROACHES. JOURNAL OF INTELLECTUAL & DEVELOPMENTAL DISABILITY, 34(1), 17–27.

- Meyer, D. J., & Vadasy, P. F. (2008). LIVING WITH A BROTHER OR SISTER WITH SPECIAL NEEDS: A BOOK FOR SIBS. University of Washington Press.

Chapter 11: Planning with Peace of Mind

- Kubler-Ross, E., & Kessler, D. (2004). ON GRIEF AND GRIEVING: FINDING THE MEANING OF GRIEF THROUGH THE FIVE STAGES OF LOSS. Scribner.

- Wright, S. (2013). SPECIAL NEEDS TRUSTS: PROTECT YOUR CHILD'S FINANCIAL FUTURE. Nolo Press.

Chapter 12: You Were Chosen for This Journey

- Siegel, D. J., & Hartzell, M. (2013). PARENTING FROM THE INSIDE OUT: HOW A DEEPER SELF-UNDERSTANDING CAN HELP YOU RAISE CHILDREN WHO THRIVE. TarcherPerigee.

- Walsch, N. D. (1995). CONVERSATIONS WITH GOD: AN UNCOMMON DIALOGUE, BOOK 1. Putnam.

- Williamson, M. (1994). A RETURN TO LOVE: REFLECTIONS ON THE PRINCIPLES OF A COURSE IN MIRACLES. HarperOne.

SECTION TWO: For Support Professionals

Chapter 13: Seeing the Individual Beyond the Label

- Ne'eman, A. (2010). LOUD HANDS: AUTISTIC PEOPLE, SPEAKING. The Autistic Press.

- Prizant, B. M. (2015). UNIQUELY HUMAN: A DIFFERENT WAY OF SEEING AUTISM. Simon & Schuster.

Chapter 14: Creating Sensory and Spirit Friendly Spaces

- Grandin, T. (2013). THE AUTISTIC BRAIN: THINKING ACROSS THE SPECTRUM. Houghton Mifflin Harcourt.

- Koenig, H. G. (2008). MEDICINE, RELIGION, AND HEALTH: WHERE SCIENCE AND SPIRITUALITY MEET. Templeton Foundation Press.

Chapter 15: Holistic Communication Tools

- Light, J., & McNaughton, D. (2012). SUPPORTING THE COMMUNICATION, LANGUAGE, AND LITERACY DEVELOPMENT OF CHILDREN WITH COMPLEX COMMUNICATION NEEDS. Paul H. Brookes Publishing Co.

Chapter 16: Being Trauma-Informed and Spiritually-Aware

- Kapp, S. K. (2020). AUTISTIC COMMUNITY AND THE NEURODIVERSITY MOVEMENT: STORIES FROM THE FRONTLINE. Palgrave Macmillan.

- van der Kolk, B. (2015). THE BODY KEEPS THE SCORE: BRAIN, MIND, AND BODY IN THE HEALING OF TRAUMA. Penguin Books.

Chapter 17: Recognizing Spiritual Intelligence

- Gardner, H. (2000). *Intelligence Reframed: Multiple Intelligences for the 21st Century*. Basic Books.
-
  Zohar, D., & Marshall, I. (2000). *SQ: Connecting with Our Spiritual Intelligence*. Bloomsbury Publishing.

Chapter 18: Serving the Family as Whole

- Siegel, D. J., & Bryson, T. P. (2011). THE WHOLE-BRAIN CHILD: 12 REVOLUTIONARY STRATEGIES TO NURTURE YOUR CHILD'S DEVELOPING MIND. Bantam.

- Turnbull, A., Turnbull, R., Erwin, E. J., Soodak, L. C., & Shogren, K. A. (2015). FAMILIES, PROFESSIONALS, AND EXCEPTIONALITY: POSITIVE OUTCOMES THROUGH PARTNERSHIPS AND TRUST. Pearson.

Chapter 19: Guiding with Meaning and Purpose

- Hagner, D., & Cooney, B. F. (2005). SELF-DETERMINATION AND CHOICE: MAKING A POSITIVE DIFFERENCE IN PEOPLE'S LIVES. Brookes Publishing.

- Shea, V. (2018). POSITIVE BEHAVIOR SUPPORT: STRATEGIES FOR TEACHERS AND PROFESSIONALS. Routledge.

Chapter 20: Sacred Structures and Routines

- Dunn, W. (2007). SUPPORTING CHILDREN TO PARTICIPATE SUCCESSFULLY IN EVERYDAY LIFE BY USING SENSORY PROCESSING KNOWLEDGE. Infants & Young Children.

- Koenig, K. P., & Rudney, S. G. (2010). PERFORMANCE CHALLENGES FOR CHILDREN AND YOUTH WITH SENSORY PROCESSING DISORDERS: A SURVEY OF PARENTS AND TEACHERS. American Journal of Occupational Therapy.

Chapter 21: Mindfulness and Grounding Practices

- Bogdashina, O. (2016). SENSORY PERCEPTUAL ISSUES IN AUTISM AND ASPERGER SYNDROME: DIFFERENT SENSORY EXPERIENCES - DIFFERENT PERCEPTUAL WORLDS. Jessica Kingsley Publishers.

- Kabat-Zinn, J. (2013). FULL CATASTROPHE LIVING: USING THE WISDOM OF YOUR BODY AND MIND TO FACE STRESS, PAIN, AND ILLNESS. Bantam Books.

Chapter 22: Developing Sacred Rapport

- Rogers, C. R. (1961). ON BECOMING A PERSON: A THERAPIST'S VIEW OF PSYCHOTHERAPY. Houghton Mifflin Harcourt.

Chapter 23: Ethical Empowerment

- Bascom, Julia. LOUD HANDS: AUTISTIC PEOPLE, SPEAKING. Autistic Self Advocacy Network, 2012.

- Kapp, Steven. AUTISM AND THE SOCIAL MODEL. Palgrave Macmillan, 2019.

- Neumeier, Sebastian. AUTISTIC COMMUNITY AND THE NEURODIVERSITY MOVEMENT. Springer, 2020.

Chapter 24: Caring for the Whole Being

- Prizant, Barry. UNIQUELY HUMAN: A DIFFERENT WAY OF SEEING AUTISM. Simon & Schuster, 2015.

- Siegel, Daniel J., and Tina Payne Bryson. THE WHOLE-BRAIN CHILD. Delacorte Press, 2011.

SECTION THREE: For Autism Advocates

Chapter 25: The Spiritual Power of Neurodiversity

- Kapp, Steven. AUTISTIC COMMUNITY AND THE NEURODIVERSITY MOVEMENT. Springer, 2020.

- Silberman, Steve. NEUROTRIBES: THE LEGACY OF AUTISM AND THE FUTURE OF NEURODIVERSITY. Avery Publishing, 2015.

Chapter 26: Centering Autistic Voices

- Bascom, Julia. LOUD HANDS: AUTISTIC PEOPLE, SPEAKING. Autistic Self Advocacy Network, 2012.

- Biklen, Douglas. AUTISM AND THE MYTH OF THE PERSON ALONE. NYU Press, 2005.

Chapter 27: Dignity for All

- Kim, Eunjung. CURATING ACCESS: DISABILITY ART ACTIVISM AND THE POLITICS OF DIGNITY. Duke University Press, 2016.

Chapter 28: Creating Sacred Inclusion

- Ault, Monica. INCLUSIVE SPIRITUALITY: EMBRACING NEURODIVERSE WORSHIP. Harmony Press, 2010.

Chapter 29: Educating with Love and Light

- Palmer, Parker J. THE COURAGE TO TEACH: EXPLORING THE INNER LANDSCAPE OF A TEACHER'S LIFE. Jossey-Bass, 1998.

Chapter 30: Language That Honors the Soul

- Biklen, Douglas. AUTISM AND THE MYTH OF THE PERSON ALONE. New York University Press, 2005.

Chapter 31: Justice as Spiritual Imperative

- Hooks, Bell. ALL ABOUT LOVE: NEW VISIONS. William Morrow, 2000.

Chapter 32: Infusing Policy with Purpose

- Taylor, Steven J. AUTISM AND THE ETHICS OF INCLUSION. Disability Studies Quarterly, 2010.

Chapter 33: Empowering the Spirit of the Advocate

- Lorde, Audre. SISTER OUTSIDER: ESSAYS AND SPEECHES. Crossing Press, 1984.

Chapter 34: Redefining Safety with Compassion

- Prizant, Barry M. UNIQUELY HUMAN: A DIFFERENT WAY OF SEEING AUTISM. Simon & Schuster, 2015.

Chapter 35: Building Conscious Communities

- Wheatley, Margaret J. TURNING TO ONE ANOTHER: SIMPLE CONVERSATIONS TO RESTORE HOPE TO THE FUTURE. Berrett-Koehler, 2002.

Chapter 36: Affirming Sacred Purpose

- Palmer, Parker J. LET YOUR LIFE SPEAK: LISTENING FOR THE VOICE OF VOCATION. Jossey-Bass, 2000.

- Vanier, Jean. BECOMING HUMAN. Paulist Press, 1998.

Glossary of Terms by Chapter

SECTION ONE: For Parents of Autistic Individuals

Chapter 1: Seeing the Divine in Your Child

- **Attunement** – Emotional or energetic sensitivity to another person's internal state.

- **Energetic Field** – The subtle emotional or spiritual atmosphere one radiates.

- **Neurodivergent** – A non-pathological variation in neurological development and functioning.

- **Presence** – The act of being emotionally, mentally, and spiritually available in the moment.

- **Sacred Lens** – A way of perceiving life or people through the perspective of spiritual meaning and value.

- **Spiritual Parenting** – A conscious, soul-based approach to raising children with attention to emotional and spiritual development.

- **Stimming** – Repetitive physical movements or sounds used by autistic individuals to self-soothe or regulate sensory input.

Chapter 2: Parenting with Presence

- **Attunement** – The emotional synchronization between caregiver and child.

- **Energetic Awareness** – The ability to sense and respond to emotional and spiritual signals.

- **Loving-Kindness** – A meditative practice of sending goodwill and compassion to self and others.

- **Mindfulness** – The practice of being fully aware and engaged in the present moment.

- **Multitasking** – Attempting to manage multiple activities at once, often reducing presence.

- **Presence** – A state of deep, conscious, and intentional awareness with another.

- **Sanctuary** – A safe, grounded space (physical or energetic) where emotional safety is fostered.

- **Self-Compassion** – The act of extending kindness and understanding to oneself during hardship.

- **Sensory Regulation** – Strategies used by individuals (consciously or unconsciously) to maintain emotional balance.

- **Task-Driven Living** – A lifestyle focused more on productivity than connection or presence.

Chapter 3: Spiritual Approaches to sensory Sensitivities

- **Aura** – The energetic field surrounding a person, often associated with emotional or spiritual state.

- **Co-Regulation** – The process by which one person supports another's nervous system through calm presence.

- **Grounding** – A practice that helps connect a person to the present moment and physical body.

- **Meltdown** – An intense response to overwhelming sensory or emotional input.

- **Sacred Space** – A designated area that promotes peace, reflection, and energetic safety.

- **Sensory Sensitivity** – Heightened or atypical response to sensory stimuli such as sound, light, texture, or smell.

- **Self-Healing Rituals** – Repetitive or calming activities that help regulate body and mind naturally.

- **Soul Listening** – Deep observation that honors emotional or energetic communication beyond words.

- **Trigger** – A specific stimulus that causes discomfort or overwhelm.

- **Weighted Blanket** – A therapeutic item designed to provide deep pressure for sensory regulation.

Chapter 4: Trusting Their Path

- **Authenticity** – The quality of being true to one's self, not shaped by external expectations.

- **Curriculum (Spiritual)** – The soul's unique path of growth, learning, and purpose in this life.

- **Discernment** – Spiritual clarity to choose what aligns with one's deeper truth or path.

- **Linear Development** – A conventional view of progress as a predictable, straight-line process.

- **Nonlinear Growth** – A pattern of learning or development marked by cycles, pauses, or reversals.

- **Path (Spiritual)** – The unique, divinely guided journey of an individual soul.

- **Sacred Surrender** – A practice of releasing control and placing trust in a higher order or plan.

- **Self-Trust** – Confidence in one's internal wisdom and ability to make aligned choices.

- **Soul Witness** – A supportive observer of another's spiritual journey, without judgment or agenda.

- **Timeline Pressure** – External societal expectation to achieve milestones by specific ages.

Chapter 5: Creating a Sacred Home Environment

- **Decompression Zone** – A calming, quiet area designed to help regulate a child's sensory system.

- **Energetic Peace** – A calm emotional and spiritual atmosphere in the home.

- **Environmental Rhythm** – The predictable flow or structure of space and time in the home.

- **Intentional Design** – The practice of arranging home environments to support well-being and purpose.

- **Sacred Sound** – Repetitive or calming sounds that carry personal or spiritual resonance.

- **Sanctuary** – A physical and emotional space of refuge, safety, and spiritual grounding.

- **Sensory Field** – The combined input of light, sound, touch, scent, and visual stimuli in a space.

- **Spiritual Anchor** – A symbol, routine, or object that provides grounding and reassurance.

- **Temple Mindset** – Viewing the home as a sacred space that nurtures soul growth and peace.

- **Visual Schedule** – A visual representation of the day's routine to aid predictability and reduce anxiety.

Chapter 6: Heart-to-Heart Communication

- **AAC (Augmentative and Alternative Communication):** Tools and methods that support or replace verbal speech, such as devices, picture boards, or apps.

- **Energetic Empathy:** The intuitive ability to sense another person's emotional or energetic state.

- **Heart-to-Heart Communication:** A spiritual approach to connecting with others through presence, intuition, and emotional attunement, rather than solely through words.

- **Intuitive Sensitivity:** The capacity to receive inner impressions or insights beyond the five senses.

- **Presence:** A mindful, calm state of being fully engaged in the current moment.

- **Sacred Ritual:** A spiritual activity or routine performed with reverence and intention.

- **Soul Cue:** A non-verbal signal or impression from another's inner self, often received through intuition.

Chapter 7: Faith, Hope, and Emotional Strength

- **Affirmation:** A positive, intentional statement spoken to reinforce belief or emotional strength.

- **Emotional Resilience:** The capacity to recover and adapt in the face of emotional challenges.

- **Faith:** A spiritual trust in the unseen order, goodness, or divine orchestration of life events.

- **Hope:** A belief in possibility, positive change, or meaningful progress even in the midst of hardship.
- **Mantra:** A word or phrase repeated for spiritual grounding, emotional focus, or meditative strength.
- **Sacred Parenting:** A mindful, spiritually-informed approach to parenting that honors the child's soul.
- **Spiritual Ritual:** A repetitive action performed with sacred intent, used to ground, uplift, or connect.

Chapter 8: Navigating the System with Grace

- **Advocacy:** Actively supporting a cause or individual's rights and needs.
- **Clarity:** A state of focused mental and spiritual understanding.
- **Discernment:** The spiritual and emotional skill of determining what is right or aligned.
- **Grace:** Calm strength and spiritual composure under pressure.
- **Mantra:** A repeated word or phrase used to focus the mind and spirit.
- **Non-Reactivity:** The ability to choose calm and deliberate responses instead of impulsive reactions.
- **Righteous Assertiveness:** Speaking boldly and truthfully with spiritual integrity.

Chapter 9: Celebrating Progress with Gratitude

- **Gratitude Ritual:** A regular practice of reflecting on or celebrating the positive aspects of one's experience.
- **Gratitude Jar:** A container used to collect written expressions of daily gratitude.
- **Gratitude Altar:** A dedicated space with symbolic items honoring growth and spiritual milestones.
- **Progress Reframing:** The act of interpreting setbacks or challenges as opportunities for spiritual growth.
- **Sacred Ceremony:** A spiritually meaningful event marking a moment of growth or transition.
- **Spiritual Memory:** The emotional imprint of being loved, celebrated, and seen through a spiritual lens.

- **Witnessing:** Being fully present to observe and honor another person's experience or transformation.

Chapter 10: Siblings and Soul Lessons

- **Affirmation:** A positive statement intended to uplift or affirm worth.

- **Reflective Dialogue:** A guided conversation aimed at exploring feelings and experiences.

- **Sacred Contract:** A spiritual belief that souls agree to specific relationships and roles before birth.

- **Sibling Ritual:** A regular activity shared between siblings that reinforces connection and bonding.

- **Soul Contract:** A metaphysical agreement between souls for mutual growth.

- **Spiritual Storytelling:** Narratives that frame life experiences within a sacred or growth-oriented lens.

  Spiritual Equality: The recognition that all souls are equally valued regardless of practical needs or roles.

Chapter 11: Planning with Peace of Mind

- **Circle of Support:** A group of trusted individuals who help ensure long-term well-being.

- **Future Anchoring:** Writing or creating messages intended to guide and reassure loved ones after your passing.

- **Legacy Planning:** Creating legal, financial, and spiritual plans to guide your child's future.

- **Sacred Care Manual:** A personalized document capturing daily routines, preferences, and spiritual practices.

- **Special Needs Trust:** A legal tool for protecting a person's eligibility for public benefits while managing financial assets.

- **Spiritual Stewardship:** Taking responsibility for another's care in a manner rooted in love and sacred intention.

- **Vision Clarity:** The process of imagining and defining what an ideal, soul-supportive future looks like.

Chapter 12: You Were Chosen for This Journey

- **Alchemy of Love:** The spiritual process of transforming fear or pain into healing through unconditional love.

- **Mirror of Purpose:** A reflective spiritual practice focused on self-affirmation and intention.

- **Parenting as Prayer:** A sacred view of caregiving as an act of devotion and spiritual alignment.

- **Presence over Perfection:** A principle emphasizing being emotionally and spiritually present rather than ideal.

- **Sacred Contract:** A belief that souls agree to certain roles and relationships before birth for mutual growth.

- **Spiritual Legacy:** The lasting energetic and emotional impact a parent leaves through love and example.

- **Spiritual Resilience:** The inner strength developed through faith-based practices and perspective.

SECTION TWO: For Support Professionals

Chapter 13: Seeing the Individual Beyond the Label

- **AAC (Augmentative and Alternative Communication):** Tools and strategies that support communication for those with speech or language challenges.

- **Energetic Hygiene:** Practices to clear and regulate one's own energy before interacting with others.

- **Non-verbal Honoring:** Valuing and respecting communication that occurs without spoken language.

- **Person-First Presence:** A mindset that sees and prioritizes the individual before any diagnosis.

- **Soul Witnessing:** A spiritual practice of acknowledging the sacred essence in another person.

- **Spiritually Grounded Practice:** An approach to professional care that integrates both technical skill and spiritual awareness.

- **Support Needs:** A respectful term describing the help an individual may require without implying deficiency.

Chapter 14: Creating Sensory and Spirit Friendly Spaces

- **Co-Regulator:** A person who helps another regulate their nervous system through calm and connected presence.

- **Energetic Tone:** The overall emotional or spiritual atmosphere of a space.

- **Regulation Tools:** Items or techniques that help balance the nervous system.

- **Ritual and Routine:** Repeated, intentional actions that bring structure and spiritual rhythm.

- **Sacred Container:** A space made safe and intentional for healing, reflection, or transformation.

- **Sensory-Friendly Design:** Environmental choices made to reduce overstimulation and enhance comfort.

- **Spiritual Inclusivity:** The act of creating space that honors diverse spiritual needs and energies.

Chapter 15: Holistic Communication Tools

- **AAC (Augmentative and Alternative Communication):** Non-spoken tools and methods used to express language.

- **Echolalia:** The repetition of words or phrases, often used to process or self-regulate.

- **Energetic Listening:** Tuning into the nonverbal emotional and spiritual signals of another person.

- **Holistic Communication:** An approach to communication that includes physical, emotional, spiritual, and energetic dimensions.

- **Sacred Listening:** Listening with full presence and spiritual openness, beyond words.

- **Self-Expression:** The act of conveying identity, emotion, or creativity through any mode of communication.

- **Scripting:** The repetition of pre-learned phrases, often used by autistic individuals to navigate social situations.

Chapter 16: Being Trauma-Informed and Spiritually-Aware

- **Energetic Sensitivity:** Heightened awareness of sensory and emotional energy in the environment.

- **Grounding Rituals:** Spiritual or sensory practices used to regulate the nervous system and restore calm.

- **Narrative Safety:** The protected freedom to tell one's own story without judgment or reinterpretation.

- **Sacred Witnessing:** Offering presence and compassion to someone's pain without attempting to fix it.

- **Sanctuary Space:** A calm, spiritually safe environment designed to support regulation and reflection.

- **Spiritual Autonomy:** The right to choose one's own spiritual beliefs, rituals, and preferences.

- **Spiritual Bypassing:** Using spiritual ideas to avoid facing emotional pain or trauma.

Chapter 17: Recognizing Spiritual Intelligence

- **Existential Questioning:** Reflecting on life's deeper meanings and spiritual truths.

- **Intuition:** The inner knowing that arises beyond rational thought.

- **Nonlinear Communication:** Expressing ideas through metaphor, symbols, or imaginative forms.

- **Sensory Sensitivity:** Heightened awareness of light, sound, touch, or energy in the environment.

- **Spiritual Intelligence:** The ability to perceive, understand, and connect with transcendent meaning.

- **Spiritual Witnessing:** Honoring another's spiritual essence without analysis or judgment.

- **Symbolic Communication:** The use of imagery, gesture, or metaphor to convey inner experience.

Chapter 18: Serving the Family as a Whole

- **Energy Mapping:** A visual tool for representing relational dynamics within the family.

- **Family Constellation:** A symbolic diagram of family members and their energetic relationships.

- **Relational Reflection:** A practice of mirroring back observed strengths in family interactions.

- **Sacred Circle of Care:** A safe and spiritually grounded space where all family members are acknowledged and supported.

- **Spiritual Cue:** A behavior or action that reflects a deeper spiritual or energetic need.

- **Team Language:** Language that reinforces collaboration and shared purpose among family members.

- **Universal Tools:** Spiritual or wellness practices that transcend specific religious traditions.

Chapter 19: Guiding with Meaning and Purpose

- **Agency:** The ability to make choices and act on one's own behalf.

- **Deficit-Based Thinking:** A mindset focused on what someone lacks rather than their strengths.

- **Encouragement with Reverence:** Supporting someone's growth while honoring their pace and nature.

- **Ritual and Rhythm:** Predictable actions that carry emotional or spiritual meaning.

- **Soul-Aligned Choice-Making:** Offering decisions that reflect an individual's authentic self.

- **Spiritual Flourishing:** Living in a way that expresses one's spiritual essence.

- **Strengths-Based Language:** Communication that emphasizes abilities over challenges.

Chapter 20: Sacred Structure and Routines

- **Collaborative Calibration:** The joint process of adjusting routines to meet individual needs.

- **Micro-Routine:** A short sequence of predictable actions designed to bring structure to a specific part of the day.

- **Rituals of Rhythm:** Symbolic or sensory practices tied to time or transition.

- **Sacred Structure:** Routine infused with intention, predictability, and emotional safety.

- **Sensory Break:** A planned pause to help regulate sensory input and maintain balance.

- **Visual Schedule:** A tool using images or symbols to communicate daily routines.

- **Wind-Down Ritual:** A consistent series of calming actions leading to rest or closure.

Chapter 21: Mindfulness and Grounding Practices

- **Active Mindfulness:** Engaging in movement or sensory activities with present-moment focus.

- **Co-Regulation:** A shared emotional experience where one person helps another return to a state of balance.

- **Grounding:** Techniques that reconnect a person to their body or present environment.

- **Mindful Moment Board:** A visual choice board that offers grounding or mindfulness activities.

- **Presence:** Being fully aware and engaged in the current moment.

- **Sensory Mindfulness:** Tuning into one's senses to support calm and focus.

- **Weighted Tools:** Items used to provide calming deep pressure input (e.g., blankets, vests).

Chapter 22: Developing Sacred Rapport

- **Co-Regulation:** The process of emotionally synchronizing with another to promote calm.

- **Energetic Safety:** A felt sense of emotional and spiritual security in a relational space.

- **Parallel Play:** Engaging in similar activities alongside another without direct interaction.

- **Ritualized Greeting:** A consistent and meaningful way to begin or end an interaction.

- **Sacred Rapport:** A soul-based connection rooted in presence, respect, and intuitive alignment.

- **Strength-Based Language:** Communication that focuses on abilities and potential rather than deficits.

- **Trust Repair:** The act of restoring safety and connection after a relational misstep.

Chapter 23: Ethical Empowerment

- **AAC (Augmentative and Alternative Communication):** Tools that help non-speaking individuals express themselves.

- **Autonomy:** The ability to make one's own choices freely.

- **Empowerment:** The process of enabling others to claim and exercise their personal authority.

- **Neurodiversity:** The concept that neurological differences are normal variations of the human experience.

- **Saviorism:** The practice of rescuing others in ways that limit their autonomy.

- **Self-Advocacy:** The skill of expressing one's needs, preferences, and rights.

- **Spiritual Identity:** A person's sense of self connected to their inner values, beliefs, or higher meaning.

Chapter 24: Caring for the Whole Being

- **Co-Regulation:** The process of helping someone regulate their emotions through your presence and behavior.

- **Energetic Exchange:** The flow of emotional and physical energy between people.

- **Holistic Care:** Support that addresses mind, body, emotions, and spirit.

- **Neurodivergent Expressions:** Natural variations in communication, behavior, and movement patterns.

- **Presence:** The state of being fully engaged, calm, and attentive in the moment.
- **Relationship-Centered Care:** Support focused on connection, mutual respect, and emotional safety.
- **Soul Expression:** The authentic way a person shows up in the world—spiritually, emotionally, and personally.

SECTION THREE: For Autism Advocates

Chapter 25: The Spiritual Power of Neurodiversity

- **Divine Blueprint:** A spiritual belief that each soul is designed with intention and purpose.
- **Energetic Regulation:** The act of using physical movement or rhythm to manage internal energy.
- **Neurodivergent:** A term describing individuals whose neurological development and function are atypical.
- **Pathologizing:** Treating a natural variation as a medical or psychological disorder.
- **Sacred Difference:** The belief that all forms of human diversity are inherently valuable and holy.
- **Soul's Journey:** A metaphysical view of life as a spiritual mission unique to each person.
- **Spiritual Ecology:** The interconnected web of all spiritual expressions within humanity.

Chapter 26: Centering Autistic Voices

- **AAC (Augmentative and Alternative Communication):** Tools that support non-verbal expression.
- **Assume Competence:** The belief that every person has intelligence and inner life, even if it's not outwardly expressed.
- **Centering:** Prioritizing the voice and experience of a group in decision-making and discourse.
- **Deficit Language:** Phrasing that frames individuals as lacking or broken.

- **Identity-First Language:** A form of description that places the identity first (e.g., "autistic person").
- **Neurodivergent:** A term describing brains that function differently from the dominant societal norm.
- **Tokenism:** Surface-level inclusion that lacks real influence or agency.

Chapter 27: Dignity for All

- **Autonomy:** The right to self-direct one's actions, choices, and body.
- **Dignity:** The inherent worth and sacredness of every person.
- **Emotional Sovereignty:** The right to express one's emotions freely and safely.
- **Neurodiversity-Affirming:** Approaches that honor neurological variation as natural and valuable.
- **Pity Paradigm:** A mindset that views disabled individuals as objects of sorrow rather than empowerment.
- **Sacred Worth:** The spiritual value attributed to every human being.
- **Trauma-Informed:** A framework that considers the impact of past trauma in care and communication.

Chapter 28: Creating Sacred Inclusion

- **AAC (Augmentative and Alternative Communication):** Tools supporting non-verbal expression.
- **Communion:** A deep spiritual connection or shared participation in the sacred.
- **Environmental Respect:** Designing physical spaces to honor sensory and neurological diversity.
- **Neurodiverse Identities:** The spectrum of neurologically varied ways of being.
- **Sacred Inclusion:** Welcoming all individuals as expressions of divine presence.
- **Sensory Regulation:** Tools and behaviors used to manage sensory input and energy levels.

- **Tokenism:** Surface-level inclusion without meaningful power-sharing or transformation.

Chapter 29: Educating with Love and Light

- **Breathwork:** A spiritual practice using intentional breathing to calm or energize
- **Love-Based Education:** Teaching rooted in empathy, respect, and connection
- **Presence:** Fully attuned, compassionate awareness in the moment
- **Soul Steward:** One who nurtures the spiritual development of others
- **Spiritually Safe Space:** An environment where all expressions of identity and emotion are honored
- **Whole-Person Learning:** Instruction that addresses emotional, spiritual, and cognitive growth
- **Wisdom-Based Curriculum:** Teaching that integrates life meaning, ethics, and inner growth

Chapter 30: Language That Honors the Soul

- **Affirming Language:** Words that support identity, dignity, and truth.
- **Communication Preferences:** The method a person prefers to use to express themselves.
- **Deficit Framing:** A way of speaking that emphasizes what a person lacks.
- **Fix-It Framework:** A mindset that views autism as a problem to be solved.
- **Inner Scripts:** Internalized language that shapes self-perception.
- **Non-Speaking Communication:** Any valid form of communication that does not rely on spoken language.
- **Sacred Accuracy:** Language that reflects both truth and spiritual reverence.

Chapter 31: Justice as Spiritual Imperative

- **Caregiver Justice:** Fair systems that support those who care for others

- **Moral Document:** A policy or law that reflects ethical and spiritual values

- **Restorative Justice:** A healing-centered approach to addressing harm

- **Sacred Disruption:** A spiritually aligned refusal to accept injustice

- **Spiritual Neglect:** The exclusion of individuals from meaningful spiritual engagement

- **Systemic Justice:** Justice implemented through institutions, policies, and systems

- **Voice Amplification:** Centering the lived experiences of marginalized individuals

Chapter 32: Infusing Policy with Purpose

- **Compliance Mentality:** A system built around obedience over understanding

- **Culturally-Informed Policy:** Guidelines that reflect diverse identities and communication needs

- **Inclusive Language:** Wording that respects and affirms all individuals

- **Purpose-Driven Policy:** Policy rooted in ethical and spiritual values, not just efficiency

- **Sacred Leadership:** Ethical decision-making aligned with spiritual principles

- **Systemic Accessibility:** The embedding of access and accommodation into core structures

- **Values-Based Budgeting:** Allocating resources based on human and spiritual priorities

Chapter 33: Empowering the Spirit of the Advocate

- **Advocacy Burnout:** Emotional and physical fatigue from sustained advocacy without proper replenishment

- **Empowerment Lens:** A framework that seeks to amplify others without controlling them

- **Inner Ecosystem:** The emotional, spiritual, and energetic well-being of the self

- **Living Prayer:** Daily actions aligned with spiritual values
- **Ripple Effect:** The idea that small acts of advocacy create wider change
- **Sacred Invitation:** A challenge or resistance that prompts deeper spiritual alignment
- **Soul-Led Advocacy:** Advocacy rooted in compassion, justice, and divine alignment

Chapter 34: Redefining Safety with Compassion

- **Compassion-Centered Safety:** An approach to safety rooted in empathy, not control
- **Co-Regulation:** A relational process where one person supports another's emotional regulation
- **Control-Based Model:** A safety model reliant on compliance, authority, and restriction
- **Relational Safety:** The experience of feeling emotionally secure in connection with others
- **Sacred Right:** A spiritually affirmed entitlement to dignity, peace, and self-determination
- **Sensory Retreat:** A designated space to reduce sensory input and restore balance
- **Spiritual Safety:** A sense of being safe in one's full humanity—body, mind, and soul

Chapter 35: Building Conscious Communities

- **Communion:** A deep spiritual connection that goes beyond surface interaction
- **Conscious Community:** A group that intentionally supports spiritual and neurodiverse inclusion
- **Mutuality:** A model of shared power and reciprocal respect
- **Restorative Circles:** A conflict resolution method based on dialogue and healing
- **Sacred Rhythm:** An individual's unique emotional, sensory, and spiritual pacing

- **Sensory-Aware Design:** Creating spaces that accommodate neurodiverse sensory needs
- **Spiritual Practice of Inclusion:** Viewing inclusion as a daily, sacred discipline

Chapter 36: Affirming Sacred Purpose

- **Affirmation:** A statement that uplifts and validates a person's identity or purpose
- **Conditional Worth:** The belief that value must be earned through actions or achievement
- **Destiny Lens:** A view that sees each life as meaningful and guided by divine purpose
- **Intrinsic Value:** Worth that is inherent and not dependent on external success
- **Sacred Service:** Support that is rooted in reverence, not ego
- **Soul-Led Growth:** Development guided by inner wisdom rather than external pressure
- **Spiritual Wholeness:** The belief that a person is complete and sacred exactly as they are

Glossary for Entire Book

- **AAC (Augmentative and Alternative Communication)** – Tools supporting non-verbal expression.

- **Active Mindfulness** – Engaging in movement or sensory activities with present-moment focus.

- **Advocacy** – Actively supporting a cause or individual's rights and needs.

- **Advocacy Burnout** – Emotional and physical fatigue from sustained advocacy without proper replenishment.

- **Affirmation** – A statement that uplifts and validates a person's identity or purpose.

- **Affirming Language** – Words that support identity, dignity, and truth.

- **Agency** – The ability to make choices and act on one's own behalf.

- **Alchemy of Love** – The spiritual process of transforming fear or pain into healing through unconditional love.

- **Assume Competence** – The belief that every person has intelligence and inner life, even if it's not outwardly expressed.

- **Attunement** – The emotional synchronization between caregiver and child.

- **Aura** – The energetic field surrounding a person, often associated with emotional or spiritual state.

- **Authenticity** – The quality of being true to one's self, not shaped by external expectations.

- **Autonomy** – The right to self-direct one's actions, choices, and body.

- **Breathwork** – A spiritual practice using intentional breathing to calm or energize.

- **Caregiver Justice** – Fair systems that support those who care for others.

- **Centering** – Prioritizing the voice and experience of a group in decision-making and discourse.

- **Circle of Support** – A group of trusted individuals who help ensure long-term well-being.

- **Clarity** – A state of focused mental and spiritual understanding.

- **Co-Regulation** – A relational process where one person supports another's emotional regulation.

- **Collaborative Calibration** – The joint process of adjusting routines to meet individual needs.

- **Communication Preferences** – The method a person prefers to use to express themselves.

- **Communion** – A deep spiritual connection that goes beyond surface interaction.

- **Compassion** – Centered Safety: An approach to safety rooted in empathy, not control.

- **Compliance Mentality** – A system built around obedience over understanding.

- **Conditional Worth** – The belief that value must be earned through actions or achievement.

- **Conscious Community** – A group that intentionally supports spiritual and neurodiverse inclusion.

- **Control** – Based Model: A safety model reliant on compliance, authority, and restriction.

- **Culturally** – Informed Policy: Guidelines that reflect diverse identities and communication needs.

- **Curriculum (Spiritual)** – The soul's unique path of growth, learning, and purpose in this life.

- **Decompression Zone** – A calming, quiet area designed to help regulate a child's sensory system.

- **Deficit** – Based Thinking: A mindset focused on what someone lacks rather than their strengths.

- **Deficit Framing** – A way of speaking that emphasizes what a person lacks.

- **Deficit Language** – Phrasing that frames individuals as lacking or broken.
- **Destiny Lens** – A view that sees each life as meaningful and guided by divine purpose.

- **Dignity** – The inherent worth and sacredness of every person.

- **Discernment** – The spiritual and emotional skill of determining what is right or aligned.

- **Divine Blueprint** – A spiritual belief that each soul is designed with intention and purpose.

- **Echolalia** – The repetition of words or phrases, often used to process or self-regulate.

- **Emotional Resilience** – The capacity to recover and adapt in the face of emotional challenges.

- **Emotional Sovereignty** – The right to express one's emotions freely and safely.

- **Empowerment** – The process of enabling others to claim and exercise their personal authority.

- **Empowerment Lens** – A framework that seeks to amplify others without controlling them.

- **Encouragement with Reverence** – Supporting someone's growth while honoring their pace and nature.

- **Energetic Awareness** – The ability to sense and respond to emotional and spiritual signals.

- **Energetic Empathy** – The intuitive ability to sense another person's emotional or energetic state.

- **Energetic Exchange** – The flow of emotional and physical energy between people.

- **Energetic Field** – The subtle emotional or spiritual atmosphere one radiates.

- **Energetic Hygiene** – Practices to clear and regulate one's own energy before interacting with others.

- **Energetic Listening** – Tuning into the nonverbal emotional and spiritual signals of another person.

- **Energetic Peace** – A calm emotional and spiritual atmosphere in the home.

- **Energetic Regulation** – The act of using physical movement or rhythm to manage internal energy.

- **Energetic Safety** – A felt sense of emotional and spiritual security in a relational space.

- **Energetic Sensitivity** – Heightened awareness of sensory and emotional energy in the environment.

- **Energetic Tone** – The overall emotional or spiritual atmosphere of a space.

- **Energy Mapping** – A visual tool for representing relational dynamics within the family.

- **Environmental Respect** – Designing physical spaces to honor sensory and neurological diversity.

- **Environmental Rhythm** – The predictable flow or structure of space and time in the home.

- **Existential Questioning** – Reflecting on life's deeper meanings and spiritual truths.

- **Faith** – A spiritual trust in the unseen order, goodness, or divine orchestration of life events.

- **Family Constellation** – A symbolic diagram of family members and their energetic relationships.

- **Fix** – It Framework: A mindset that views autism as a problem to be solved.

- **Future Anchoring** – Writing or creating messages intended to guide and reassure loved ones after your passing.

- **Grace** – Calm strength and spiritual composure under pressure.

- **Gratitude Altar** – A dedicated space with symbolic items honoring growth and spiritual milestones.

- **Gratitude Jar** – A container used to collect written expressions of daily gratitude.

- **Gratitude Ritual** – A regular practice of reflecting on or celebrating the positive aspects of one's experience.

- **Grounding** – Techniques that reconnect a person to their body or present environment.

- **Grounding Rituals** – Spiritual or sensory practices used to regulate the nervous system and restore calm.

- **Heart** – to-Heart Communication: A spiritual approach to connecting with others through presence, intuition, and emotional attunement, rather than solely through words.

- **Holistic Care** – Support that addresses mind, body, emotions, and spirit.

- **Holistic Communication** – An approach to communication that includes physical, emotional, spiritual, and energetic dimensions.

- **Hope** – A belief in possibility, positive change, or meaningful progress even in the midst of hardship.

- **Identity** – First Language: A form of description that places the identity first (e.g., "autistic person").

- **Inclusive Language** – Wording that respects and affirms all individuals.

- **Inner Ecosystem** – The emotional, spiritual, and energetic well-being of the self.

- **Inner Scripts** – Internalized language that shapes self-perception.

- **Intentional Design** – The practice of arranging home environments to support well-being and purpose.

- **Intrinsic Value** – Worth that is inherent and not dependent on external success.

- **Intuition** – The inner knowing that arises beyond rational thought.

- **Intuitive Sensitivity** – The capacity to receive inner impressions or insights beyond the five senses.

- **Legacy Planning** – Creating legal, financial, and spiritual plans to guide your child's future.

- **Linear Development** – A conventional view of progress as a predictable, straight-line process.

- **Living Prayer** – Daily actions aligned with spiritual values.

- **Love** – Based Education: Teaching rooted in empathy, respect, and connection.

- **Loving** – Kindness – A meditative practice of sending goodwill and compassion to self and others.

- **Mantra** – A repeated word or phrase used to focus the mind and spirit.

- **Meltdown** – An intense response to overwhelming sensory or emotional input.

- **Micro-Routine** – A short sequence of predictable actions designed to bring structure to a specific part of the day.

- **Mindful Moment Board** – A visual choice board that offers grounding or mindfulness activities.

- **Mindfulness** – The practice of being fully aware and engaged in the present moment.

- **Mirror of Purpose** – A reflective spiritual practice focused on self-affirmation and intention.

- **Moral Document** – A policy or law that reflects ethical and spiritual values.

- **Multitasking** – Attempting to manage multiple activities at once, often reducing presence.

- **Mutuality** – A model of shared power and reciprocal respect.

- **Narrative Safety** – The protected freedom to tell one's own story without judgment or reinterpretation.

- **Neurodivergent** – A term describing brains that function differently from the dominant societal norm.

- **Neurodivergent Expressions** – Natural variations in communication, behavior, and movement patterns.

- **Neurodiverse Identities** – The spectrum of neurologically varied ways of being.

- **Neurodiversity** – Affirming: Approaches that honor neurological variation as natural and valuable.

- **Non-Speaking Communication** – Any valid form of communication that does not rely on spoken language.

- **Nonlinear Communication** – Expressing ideas through metaphor, symbols, or imaginative forms.

- **Nonlinear Growth** – A pattern of learning or development marked by cycles, pauses, or reversals.

- **Parallel Play** – Engaging in similar activities alongside another without direct interaction.

- **Parenting as Prayer** – A sacred view of caregiving as an act of devotion and spiritual alignment.

- **Path (Spiritual)** – The unique, divinely guided journey of an individual soul.

- **Pathologizing** – Treating a natural variation as a medical or psychological disorder.

- **Person-First Presence** –: A mindset that sees and prioritizes the individual before any diagnosis.

- **Pity Paradigm** – A mindset that views disabled individuals as objects of sorrow rather than empowerment.

- **Presence** – Fully attuned, compassionate awareness in the moment.

- **Presence over Perfection** – A principle emphasizing being emotionally and spiritually present rather than ideal.

- **Progress Reframing** – The act of interpreting setbacks or challenges as opportunities for spiritual growth.

- **Purpose** – Driven Policy: Policy rooted in ethical and spiritual values, not just efficiency.

- **Reflective Dialogue** – A guided conversation aimed at exploring feelings and experiences.

- **Regulation Tools** – Items or techniques that help balance the nervous system.

- **Relational Reflection** – A practice of mirroring back observed strengths in family interactions.

- **Relational Safety** – The experience of feeling emotionally secure in connection with others.

- **Relationship-Centered Care** – Support focused on connection, mutual respect, and emotional safety.

- **Restorative Circles** – A conflict resolution method based on dialogue and healing.

- **Restorative Justice** – A healing-centered approach to addressing harm.

- **Righteous Assertiveness** – Speaking boldly and truthfully with spiritual integrity.

- **Ripple Effect** – The idea that small acts of advocacy create wider change.

- **Ritual and Rhythm** – Predictable actions that carry emotional or spiritual meaning.

- **Ritual and Routine** – Repeated, intentional actions that bring structure and spiritual rhythm.

- **Ritualized Greeting** – A consistent and meaningful way to begin or end an interaction.
- **Rituals of Rhythm** – Symbolic or sensory practices tied to time or transition.
- **Sacred Accuracy** – Language that reflects both truth and spiritual reverence.
- **Sacred Care Manual** – A personalized document capturing daily routines, preferences, and spiritual practices.
- **Sacred Ceremony** – A spiritually meaningful event marking a moment of growth or transition.
- **Sacred Circle of Care** – A safe and spiritually grounded space where all family members are acknowledged and supported.
- **Sacred Container** – A space made safe and intentional for healing, reflection, or transformation.
- **Sacred Contract** – A belief that souls agree to certain roles and relationships before birth for mutual growth.
- **Sacred Difference** – The belief that all forms of human diversity are inherently valuable and holy.
- **Sacred Disruption** – A spiritually aligned refusal to accept injustice.
- **Sacred Inclusion** – Welcoming all individuals as expressions of divine presence.
- **Sacred Invitation** – A challenge or resistance that prompts deeper spiritual alignment.
- **Sacred Leadership** – Ethical decision-making aligned with spiritual principles.
- **Sacred Lens** – A way of perceiving life or people through the perspective of spiritual meaning and value.
- **Sacred Listening** – Listening with full presence and spiritual openness, beyond words.
- **Sacred Parenting** – A mindful, spiritually-informed approach to parenting that honors the child's soul.
- **Sacred Rapport** – A soul-based connection rooted in presence, respect, and intuitive alignment.

- **Sacred Rhythm** – An individual's unique emotional, sensory, and spiritual pacing
- **Sacred Right** – A spiritually affirmed entitlement to dignity, peace, and self-determination
- **Sacred Ritual** – A spiritual activity or routine performed with reverence and intention.
- **Sacred Service** – Support that is rooted in reverence, not ego
- **Sacred Sound** – Repetitive or calming sounds that carry personal or spiritual resonance.
- **Sacred Space** – A designated area that promotes peace, reflection, and energetic safety.
- **Sacred Structure** – Routine infused with intention, predictability, and emotional safety.
- **Sacred Surrender** – A practice of releasing control and placing trust in a higher order or plan.
- **Sacred Witnessing** – Offering presence and compassion to someone's pain without attempting to fix it.
- **Sacred Worth** – The spiritual value attributed to every human being.
- **Sanctuary** – A physical and emotional space of refuge, safety, and spiritual grounding.
- **Sanctuary Space** – A calm, spiritually safe environment designed to support regulation and reflection.
- **Saviorism** – The practice of rescuing others in ways that limit their autonomy.
- **Scripting** – The repetition of pre-learned phrases, often used by autistic individuals to navigate social situations.
- **Self- Advocacy** - The skill of expressing one's needs, preferences, and rights.
- **Sensory-Aware Design** – Creating spaces that accommodate neurodiverse sensory needs.
- **Sensory Break** – A planned pause to help regulate sensory input and maintain balance.
- **Sensory Field** – The combined input of light, sound, touch, scent, and visual stimuli in a space.

- **Sensory Mindfulness** – Tuning into one's senses to support calm and focus.

- **Sensory Regulation** – Tools and behaviors used to manage sensory input and energy levels.

- **Sensory Retreat** – A designated space to reduce sensory input and restore balance.

- **Sensory Sensitivity** – Heightened awareness of light, sound, touch, or energy in the environment.

- **Sibling Ritual** – A regular activity shared between siblings that reinforces connection and bonding.

- **Soul** – Led Growth: Development guided by inner wisdom rather than external pressure.

- **Soul Contract** – A metaphysical agreement between souls for mutual growth.

- **Soul Cue** – A non-verbal signal or impression from another's inner self, often received through intuition.

- **Soul Expression** – The authentic way a person shows up in the world – spiritually, emotionally, and personally.

- **Soul Listening** – Deep observation that honors emotional or energetic communication beyond words.

- **Soul Steward** – One who nurtures the spiritual development of others.

- **Soul Witness** – A supportive observer of another's spiritual journey, without judgment or agenda.

- **Soul Witnessing** – A spiritual practice of acknowledging the sacred essence in another person.

- **Soul's Journey** – A metaphysical view of life as a spiritual mission unique to each person.

- **Special Needs Trust** – A legal tool for protecting a person's eligibility for public benefits while managing financial assets.

- **Spiritual Anchor** – A symbol, routine, or object that provides grounding and reassurance.

- **Spiritual Autonomy** – The right to choose one's own spiritual beliefs, rituals, and preferences.

- **Spiritual Bypassing** – Using spiritual ideas to avoid facing emotional pain or trauma.

- **Spiritual Cue** – A behavior or action that reflects a deeper spiritual or energetic need.

- **Spiritual Ecology** – The interconnected web of all spiritual expressions within humanity.

- **Spiritual Equality** – The recognition that all souls are equally valued regardless of practical needs or roles.

- **Spiritual Flourishing** – Living in a way that expresses one's spiritual essence.

- **Spiritual Identity** – A person's sense of self connected to their inner values, beliefs, or higher meaning.

- **Spiritual Inclusivity** – The act of creating space that honors diverse spiritual needs and energies.

- **Spiritual Intelligence** – The ability to perceive, understand, and connect with transcendent meaning.

- **Spiritual Legacy** – The lasting energetic and emotional impact a parent leaves through love and example.

- **Spiritual Memory** – The emotional imprint of being loved, celebrated, and seen through a spiritual lens.

- **Spiritual Neglect** – The exclusion of individuals from meaningful spiritual engagement.

- **Spiritual Parenting** – A conscious, soul-based approach to raising children with attention to emotional and spiritual development.

- **Spiritual Practice of Inclusion** – Viewing inclusion as a daily, sacred discipline.

- **Spiritual Resilience** – The inner strength developed through faith-based practices and perspective.

- **Spiritual Ritual** – A repetitive action performed with sacred intent, used to ground, uplift, or connect.

- **Spiritual Safety** – A sense of being safe in one's full humanity—body, mind, and soul.

- **Spiritual Stewardship** – Taking responsibility for another's care in a manner rooted in love and sacred intention.

- **Spiritual Storytelling** – Narratives that frame life experiences within a sacred or growth-oriented lens.

- **Spiritual Wholeness** – The belief that a person is complete and sacred exactly as they are.

- **Spiritual Witnessing** – Honoring another's spiritual essence without analysis or judgment.

- **Spiritually Grounded Practice** – An approach to professional care that integrates both technical skill and spiritual awareness.

- **Spiritually Safe Space** – An environment where all expressions of identity and emotion are honored.

- **Stimming** – Repetitive physical movements or sounds used by autistic individuals to self-soothe or regulate sensory input.

- **Strength** – Based Language: Communication that focuses on abilities and potential rather than deficits.

- **Strengths** – Based Language: Communication that emphasizes abilities over challenges.

- **Support Needs** – A respectful term describing the help an individual may require without implying deficiency.

- **Symbolic Communication** – The use of imagery, gesture, or metaphor to convey inner experience.

- **Systemic Accessibility** – The embedding of access and accommodation into core structures.

- **Systemic Justice** – Justice implemented through institutions, policies, and systems.

- **Task-Driven Living** – A lifestyle focused more on productivity than connection or presence.

- **Team Language** – Language that reinforces collaboration and shared purpose among family members.

- **Temple Mindset** – Viewing the home as a sacred space that nurtures soul growth and peace.

- **Timeline Pressure** – External societal expectation to achieve milestones by specific ages.

- **Tokenism** – Surface-level inclusion without meaningful power-sharing or transformation.

- **Trauma** – Informed: A framework that considers the impact of past trauma in care and communication.

- **Trigger** – A specific stimulus that causes discomfort or overwhelm.

- **Trust Repair** – The act of restoring safety and connection after a relational misstep.

- **Universal Tools** – Spiritual or wellness practices that transcend specific religious traditions.

- **Values** – Based Budgeting: Allocating resources based on human and spiritual priorities.

- **Vision Clarity** – The process of imagining and defining what an ideal, soul-supportive future looks like.

- **Visual Schedule** – A tool using images or symbols to communicate daily routines.

- **Voice Amplification** – Centering the lived experiences of marginalized individuals.

- **Weighted Blanket** – A therapeutic item designed to provide deep pressure for sensory regulation.

- **Weighted Tools** – Items used to provide calming deep pressure input (e.g., blankets, vests).

- **Whole** – Person Learning: Instruction that addresses emotional, spiritual, and cognitive growth.

- **Wind** – Down Ritual: A consistent series of calming actions leading to rest or closure.

- **Wisdom** – Based Curriculum: Teaching that integrates life meaning, ethics, and inner growth.

- **Witnessing** – Being fully present to observe and honor another person's experience or transformation.

NOTES:

Suggested Reading List

SECTION ONE: For Parents of Autistic Individuals

Chapter 1: Seeing the Divine in Your Child

- Goleman, Daniel. EMOTIONAL INTELLIGENCE. Bantam, 1995.
- Tsabary, Shefali. THE AWAKENED FAMILY. Penguin, 2016.
- Maté, Gabor & Neufeld, Gordon. HOLD ON TO YOUR KIDS. Ballantine Books, 2004.
- Cohen, Deborah. PARENTING OUTSIDE THE LINES. Harper Wave, 2020.
- Kabat-Zinn, Myla & Jon. EVERYDAY BLESSINGS: THE INNER WORK OF MINDFUL PARENTING. Hachette, 2014.
- Hart, Tobin. THE SECRET SPIRITUAL WORLD OF CHILDREN. Inner Ocean, 2003.
- Sinetar, Marsha. ORDINARY PEOPLE AS MONKS AND MYSTICS. Paulist Press, 1986.

Chapter 2: Parenting with Presence

- Tolle, Eckhart. THE POWER OF NOW. New World Library, 1999.
- Siegel, Daniel J. THE MINDFUL BRAIN. W. W. Norton & Company, 2007.
- Neff, Kristin. SELF-COMPASSION. William Morrow, 2011.
- Delahooke, Mona. BEYOND BEHAVIORS. PESI Publishing, 2019.
- Greenspan, Stanley & Wieder, Serena. ENGAGING AUTISM. Da Capo Press, 2006.
- Kabat-Zinn, Jon. WHEREVER YOU GO, THERE YOU ARE. Hachette, 1994.
- Chödrön, Pema. WHEN THINGS FALL APART. Shambhala, 1997.

Chapter 3: Spiritual Approaches to Sensory Sensitivities

- Grandin, Temple. THE AUTISTIC BRAIN. Houghton Mifflin Harcourt, 2013.

- Delahooke, Mona. BEYOND BEHAVIORS. PESI Publishing, 2019.

- Bogdashina, Olga. SENSORY PERCEPTUAL ISSUES IN AUTISM. Jessica Kingsley, 2016.

- Siegel, Daniel & Bryson, Tina Payne. THE POWER OF SHOWING UP. Ballantine Books, 2020.

- Chopra, Deepak. THE BOOK OF SECRETS. Harmony, 2004.

- Hart, Tobin. THE SECRET SPIRITUAL WORLD OF CHILDREN. Inner Ocean, 2003.

- Kranowitz, Carol. THE OUT-OF-SYNC CHILD. Penguin, 2005.

Chapter 4: Trusting Their Path

- Neufeld, Gordon, & Maté, Gabor. HOLD ON TO YOUR KIDS. Ballantine Books, 2004.

- Delahooke, Mona. BEYOND BEHAVIORS. PESI Publishing, 2019.

- Tsabary, Shefali. THE AWAKENED FAMILY. TarcherPerigee, 2016.

- Walsch, Neale Donald. CONVERSATIONS WITH GOD FOR PARENTS. Hampton Roads, 1999.

- Palmer, Parker. LET YOUR LIFE SPEAK. Jossey-Bass, 2000.

- Rohr, Richard. EVERYTHING BELONGS: THE GIFT OF CONTEMPLATIVE PRAYER. Crossroad, 1999.

- Nhat Hanh, Thich. PEACE IS EVERY STEP. Bantam, 1991.

Chapter 5: Creating a Sacred Home Environment

- Ayres, A. Jean. SENSORY INTEGRATION AND THE CHILD. Western Psychological Services, 2005.

- Bogdashina, Olga. SENSORY PERCEPTUAL ISSUES IN AUTISM AND ASPERGER SYNDROME. Jessica Kingsley, 2016.

- Grandin, Temple. THE AUTISTIC BRAIN. Houghton Mifflin Harcourt, 2013.

- Kranowitz, Carol Stock. THE OUT-OF-SYNC CHILD. Penguin, 2005.

- Siegel, Daniel J., and Bryson, Tina Payne. THE WHOLE-BRAIN CHILD. Random House, 2016.

- Healy, Jane M. FAILURE TO CONNECT. Simon & Schuster, 1998.

- Nhat Hanh, Thich. MAKING SPACE: CREATING A HOME MEDITATION PRACTICE. Parallax Press, 2011.

Chapter 6: Heart-to-Heart Communication

- Siegel, Daniel J., & Bryson, Tina Payne. THE WHOLE-BRAIN CHILD: 12 REVOLUTIONARY STRATEGIES TO NURTURE YOUR CHILD'S DEVELOPING MIND. Bantam Books, 2010.

- Prizant, Barry M. UNIQUELY HUMAN: A DIFFERENT WAY OF SEEING AUTISM. Simon & Schuster, 2015.

- Tsabary, Shefali. THE AWAKENED FAMILY: A REVOLUTION IN PARENTING. Penguin Books, 2016.

- Orloff, Judith. THE EMPATH'S SURVIVAL GUIDE: LIFE STRATEGIES FOR SENSITIVE PEOPLE. Sounds True, 2017.

- Stiffelman, Susan. PARENTING WITH PRESENCE: PRACTICES FOR RAISING CONSCIOUS, CONFIDENT, CARING KIDS. New World Library, 2015.

- Thomas, Gary. SACRED PARENTING: HOW RAISING CHILDREN SHAPES OUR SOULS. Zondervan, 2005.

- Harris, Lee. ENERGY SPEAKS: MESSAGES FROM SPIRIT ON LIVING, LOVING, AND AWAKENING. New World Library, 2019.

Chapter 7: Faith, Hope, and Emotional Strength

- Neff, Kristin. SELF-COMPASSION: THE PROVEN POWER OF BEING KIND TO YOURSELF. William Morrow, 2011.

- Brown, Brené. RISING STRONG: HOW THE ABILITY TO RESET TRANSFORMS THE WAY WE LIVE, LOVE, PARENT, AND LEAD. Spiegel & Grau, 2015.

- Tsabary, Shefali. THE CONSCIOUS PARENT: TRANSFORMING OURSELVES, EMPOWERING OUR CHILDREN. Namaste Publishing, 2010.

- Van Der Kolk, Bessel. THE BODY KEEPS THE SCORE: BRAIN, MIND, AND BODY IN THE HEALING OF TRAUMA. Viking, 2014.

- Miller, Lisa. THE SPIRITUAL CHILD: THE NEW SCIENCE ON PARENTING FOR HEALTH AND LIFELONG THRIVING. St. Martin's Press, 2015.

- Thomas, Gary. SACRED PARENTING: HOW RAISING CHILDREN SHAPES OUR SOULS. Zondervan, 2005.

- Chödrön, Pema. WHEN THINGS FALL APART: HEART ADVICE FOR DIFFICULT TIMES. Shambhala Publications, 1997.

Chapter 8: Navigating the System with Grace

- Nhat Hanh, Thich. CREATING TRUE PEACE: ENDING VIOLENCE IN YOURSELF, YOUR FAMILY, YOUR COMMUNITY, AND THE WORLD. Free Press, 2002.

- Kabat-Zinn, Jon. FULL CATASTROPHE LIVING: USING THE WISDOM OF YOUR BODY AND MIND TO FACE STRESS, PAIN, AND ILLNESS. Bantam, 2013.

- Greene, Ross W., & Ablon, J. Stuart. TREATING EXPLOSIVE KIDS: THE COLLABORATIVE PROBLEM-SOLVING APPROACH. Guilford Press, 2006.

- Wright, Peter W. D., & Wright, Pamela Darr. WRIGHTSLAW: FROM EMOTIONS TO ADVOCACY – THE SPECIAL EDUCATION SURVIVAL GUIDE. Harbor House Law Press, 2006.

- Siegel, Daniel J. THE POWER OF SHOWING UP: HOW PARENTAL PRESENCE SHAPES WHO OUR KIDS BECOME AND HOW THEIR BRAINS GET WIRED. Ballantine Books, 2020.

- Williamson, Marianne. A RETURN TO LOVE: REFLECTIONS ON THE PRINCIPLES OF A COURSE IN MIRACLES. HarperOne, 1992.

- Lerner, Harriet. THE DANCE OF CONNECTION: HOW TO TALK TO SOMEONE WHEN YOU'RE MAD, HURT, SCARED, FRUSTRATED, INSULTED, BETRAYED, OR DESPERATE. Harper, 2001.

Chapter 9: Celebrating Progress with Gratitude

- Emmons, Robert A. THANKS! HOW PRACTICING GRATITUDE CAN MAKE YOU HAPPIER. Houghton Mifflin Harcourt, 2007.

- Kushner, Harold S. WHEN BAD THINGS HAPPEN TO GOOD PEOPLE. Schocken Books, 1981.

- Siegel, Daniel J., & Bryson, Tina Payne. THE POWER OF SHOWING UP: HOW PARENTAL PRESENCE SHAPES WHO OUR KIDS BECOME AND HOW THEIR BRAINS GET WIRED. Ballantine Books, 2020.

- Nhat Hanh, Thich. PEACE IS EVERY STEP: THE PATH OF MINDFULNESS IN EVERYDAY LIFE. Bantam, 1991.

- Sacks, Jonathan. CELEBRATING LIFE: FINDING HAPPINESS IN UNEXPECTED PLACES. Continuum, 2000.

- Voskamp, Ann. ONE THOUSAND GIFTS: A DARE TO LIVE FULLY RIGHT WHERE YOU ARE. Zondervan, 2010.

- O'Donohue, John. TO BLESS THE SPACE BETWEEN US: A BOOK OF BLESSINGS. Doubleday, 2008.

Chapter 10: Siblings and Soul Lessons

- Chopra, Deepak. THE SEVEN SPIRITUAL LAWS FOR PARENTS: GUIDING YOUR CHILDREN TO SUCCESS AND FULFILLMENT. Harmony Books, 1997.

- Glasberg, Barbara A. BROTHERS, SISTERS, AND AUTISM: A PARENT'S GUIDE TO SUPPORTING SIBLINGS. Woodbine House, 2000.

- Meyer, Donald J., & Vadasy, Patricia F. LIVING WITH A BROTHER OR SISTER WITH SPECIAL NEEDS: A BOOK FOR SIBS. University of Washington Press, 2008.

- Lobdell, Claire. DIFFERENT LIKE ME: A BOOK FOR KIDS ABOUT UNDERSTANDING AUTISM SPECTRUM DISORDERS. Future Horizons, 2009.

- Harris, Sandra L., & Glasberg, Barry. SIBLINGS OF CHILDREN WITH AUTISM: A GUIDE FOR FAMILIES. Woodbine House, 2003.

- Dacey, John, & Fiore, Lisa. YOUR ANXIOUS CHILD: HOW PARENTS AND TEACHERS CAN RELIEVE ANXIETY IN CHILDREN. Jossey-Bass, 2000.

- Staub, Debbie. WE'LL PAINT THE OCTOPUS RED. Woodbine House, 1998.

Chapter 11: Planning with Peace of Mind

- Wright, Stephen. SPECIAL NEEDS TRUSTS: PROTECT YOUR CHILD'S FINANCIAL FUTURE. Nolo Press, 2013.

- Kubler-Ross, Elisabeth, & Kessler, David. ON GRIEF AND GRIEVING: FINDING THE MEANING OF GRIEF THROUGH THE FIVE STAGES OF LOSS. Scribner, 2004.

- Harris, Sandra L. SIBLINGS OF CHILDREN WITH AUTISM: A GUIDE FOR FAMILIES. Woodbine House, 2003.

- Mount, Laurie. ESTATE PLANNING FOR SPECIAL NEEDS FAMILIES. Self-published, 2015.

- Trachtman, Laurie. THE SPECIAL NEEDS PLANNING GUIDE: HOW TO PREPARE FOR EVERY STAGE OF YOUR CHILD'S LIFE. Brookes Publishing, 2017.

- Nouwen, Henri J.M. LIFE OF THE BELOVED: SPIRITUAL LIVING IN A SECULAR WORLD. Crossroad Publishing, 1992.

- Siegel, Daniel J., & Bryson, Tina Payne. THE YES BRAIN: HOW TO CULTIVATE COURAGE, CURIOSITY, AND RESILIENCE IN YOUR CHILD. Random House, 2018.

Chapter 12: You Were Chosen for This Journey

- Siegel, Daniel J., & Hartzell, Mary. PARENTING FROM THE INSIDE OUT: HOW A DEEPER SELF-UNDERSTANDING CAN HELP YOU RAISE CHILDREN WHO THRIVE. TarcherPerigee, 2013.

- Williamson, Marianne. A RETURN TO LOVE: REFLECTIONS ON THE PRINCIPLES OF A COURSE IN MIRACLES. HarperOne, 1994.

- Walsch, Neale Donald. CONVERSATIONS WITH GOD: AN UNCOMMON DIALOGUE, BOOK 1. Putnam, 1995.

- Kornfield, Jack. THE WISE HEART: A GUIDE TO THE UNIVERSAL TEACHINGS OF BUDDHIST PSYCHOLOGY. Bantam, 2009.

- Palmer, Parker J. LET YOUR LIFE SPEAK: LISTENING FOR THE VOICE OF VOCATION. Jossey-Bass, 2000.

- Chodron, Pema. WHEN THINGS FALL APART: HEART ADVICE FOR DIFFICULT TIMES. Shambhala Publications, 1997.

- Nhat Hanh, Thich. PEACE IS EVERY STEP: THE PATH OF MINDFULNESS IN EVERYDAY LIFE. Bantam, 1992.

SECTION TWO: For Support Professionals

Chapter 13: Seeing the Individual Beyond the Label

- Prizant, Barry M. UNIQUELY HUMAN: A DIFFERENT WAY OF SEEING AUTISM. Simon & Schuster, 2015.

- Ne'eman, Ari. LOUD HANDS: AUTISTIC PEOPLE, SPEAKING. The Autistic Press, 2010.

- Notbohm, Ellen. TEN THINGS EVERY CHILD WITH AUTISM WISHES YOU KNEW. Future Horizons, 2005.

- Robison, John Elder. LOOK ME IN THE EYE: MY LIFE WITH ASPERGER'S. Crown, 2007.

- Silberman, Steve. NEUROTRIBES: THE LEGACY OF AUTISM AND THE FUTURE OF NEURODIVERSITY. Avery, 2015.

- Grandin, Temple. THE AUTISTIC BRAIN: THINKING ACROSS THE SPECTRUM. Mariner Books, 2014.

- Rossetti, Zachariah J. BEYOND BEHAVIOR: SUPPORTING CHILDREN AND YOUTH WITH AUTISM IN INCLUSIVE CLASSROOMS. Brookes Publishing, 2018.

Chapter 14: Creating Sensory and Spirit Friendly Spaces

- Grandin, Temple. THE AUTISTIC BRAIN: THINKING ACROSS THE SPECTRUM. Houghton Mifflin Harcourt, 2013.

- Koenig, Harold G. MEDICINE, RELIGION, AND HEALTH: WHERE SCIENCE AND SPIRITUALITY MEET. Templeton Foundation Press, 2008.

- Dunn, Winnie. LIVING SENSATIONALLY: UNDERSTANDING YOUR SENSES. Jessica Kingsley Publishers, 2008.

- Kranowitz, Carol Stock. THE OUT-OF-SYNC CHILD: RECOGNIZING AND COPING WITH SENSORY PROCESSING DISORDER. TarcherPerigee, 2005.

- Delahooke, Mona. BEYOND BEHAVIORS: USING BRAIN SCIENCE AND COMPASSION TO UNDERSTAND AND SOLVE CHILDREN'S BEHAVIORAL CHALLENGES. PESI Publishing, 2019.

- Van Der Kolk, Bessel. THE BODY KEEPS THE SCORE: BRAIN, MIND, AND BODY IN THE HEALING OF TRAUMA. Penguin Books, 2014.

- Miller, Lucy Jane. SENSATIONAL KIDS: HOPE AND HELP FOR CHILDREN WITH SENSORY PROCESSING DISORDER. TarcherPerigee, 2006.

Chapter 15: Holistic Communication Tools

- Light, Janice, & McNaughton, David. SUPPORTING THE COMMUNICATION, LANGUAGE, AND LITERACY DEVELOPMENT OF CHILDREN WITH COMPLEX COMMUNICATION NEEDS. Paul H. Brookes, 2012.

- Prizant, Barry M. UNIQUELY HUMAN: A DIFFERENT WAY OF SEEING AUTISM. Simon & Schuster, 2015.

- Notbohm, Ellen. TEN THINGS EVERY CHILD WITH AUTISM WISHES YOU KNEW. Future Horizons, 2005.

- Grandin, Temple. THINKING IN PICTURES: MY LIFE WITH AUTISM. Vintage, 2006.

- Bogdashina, Olga. COMMUNICATION ISSUES IN AUTISM AND ASPERGER SYNDROME. Jessica Kingsley Publishers, 2005.

- Attwood, Tony. THE COMPLETE GUIDE TO ASPERGER'S SYNDROME. Jessica Kingsley Publishers, 2006.

- Charlton, James I. NOTHING ABOUT US WITHOUT US: DISABILITY OPPRESSION AND EMPOWERMENT. University of California Press, 1998.

Chapter 16: Being Trauma-Informed and Spiritually-Aware

- van der Kolk, Bessel. THE BODY KEEPS THE SCORE: BRAIN, MIND, AND BODY IN THE HEALING OF TRAUMA. Penguin Books, 2015.

- Kapp, Steven K. AUTISTIC COMMUNITY AND THE NEURODIVERSITY MOVEMENT: STORIES FROM THE FRONTLINE. Palgrave Macmillan, 2020.

- Herman, Judith L. TRAUMA AND RECOVERY: THE AFTERMATH OF VIOLENCE—FROM DOMESTIC ABUSE TO POLITICAL TERROR.

Basic Books, 2015.

- Levine, Peter A. WAKING THE TIGER: HEALING TRAUMA. North Atlantic Books, 1997.

- Siegel, Daniel J. THE WHOLE-BRAIN CHILD: 12 REVOLUTIONARY STRATEGIES TO NURTURE YOUR CHILD'S DEVELOPING MIND. Bantam, 2011.

- Mate, Gabor. IN THE REALM OF HUNGRY GHOSTS: CLOSE ENCOUNTERS WITH ADDICTION. North Atlantic Books, 2008.

- Rothschild, Babette. THE BODY REMEMBERS: THE PSYCHOPHYSIOLOGY OF TRAUMA AND TRAUMA TREATMENT. W. W. Norton & Company, 2000.

Chapter 17: Recognizing Spiritual Intelligence

- Gardner, Howard. INTELLIGENCE REFRAMED: MULTIPLE INTELLIGENCES FOR THE 21ST CENTURY. Basic Books, 2000.

- Zohar, Danah, & Marshall, Ian. SQ: CONNECTING WITH OUR SPIRITUAL INTELLIGENCE. Bloomsbury, 2000.

- Chopra, Deepak. THE BOOK OF SECRETS: UNLOCKING THE HIDDEN DIMENSIONS OF YOUR LIFE. Harmony, 2004.

- Siegel, Daniel J. MINDSIGHT: THE NEW SCIENCE OF PERSONAL TRANSFORMATION. Bantam, 2010.

- Van der Kolk, Bessel. THE BODY KEEPS THE SCORE. Penguin Books, 2015.

- Hart, Toby. FROM INFORMATION TO TRANSFORMATION: EDUCATION FOR THE EVOLUTION OF CONSCIOUSNESS. Peter Lang Publishing, 2001.

- Myss, Caroline. ANATOMY OF THE SPIRIT: THE SEVEN STAGES OF POWER AND HEALING. Three Rivers Press, 1996.

Chapter 18: Serving the Family as a Whole

- Turnbull, Ann, et al. FAMILIES, PROFESSIONALS, AND EXCEPTIONALITY: POSITIVE OUTCOMES THROUGH PARTNERSHIPS AND TRUST. Pearson, 2015.

- Siegel, Daniel J., & Bryson, Tina Payne. THE WHOLE-BRAIN CHILD. Bantam, 2011.

- Neufeld, Gordon, & Maté, Gabor. HOLD ON TO YOUR KIDS: WHY PARENTS NEED TO MATTER MORE THAN PEERS. Ballantine Books, 2006.

- Hart, Toby. FROM INFORMATION TO TRANSFORMATION. Peter Lang Publishing, 2001.

- Cozolino, Louis. THE NEUROSCIENCE OF HUMAN RELATIONSHIPS. Norton, 2014.

- Kabat-Zinn, Jon. EVERYDAY BLESSINGS: THE INNER WORK OF MINDFUL PARENTING. Hachette Books, 2014.

- Faber, Adele, & Mazlish, Elaine. HOW TO TALK SO KIDS WILL LISTEN & LISTEN SO KIDS WILL TALK. Scribner, 2012.

Chapter 19: Guiding with Meaning and Purpose

- Shea, Valerie. POSITIVE BEHAVIOR SUPPORT: STRATEGIES FOR TEACHERS AND PROFESSIONALS. Routledge, 2018.

- Hagner, David, & Cooney, Brian. SELF-DETERMINATION AND CHOICE. Brookes Publishing, 2005.

- Sacks, Oliver. AN ANTHROPOLOGIST ON MARS. Knopf, 1995.

- Robison, John Elder. LOOK ME IN THE EYE: MY LIFE WITH ASPERGER'S. Crown, 2007.

- Siegel, Daniel J. MINDSIGHT: THE NEW SCIENCE OF PERSONAL TRANSFORMATION. Bantam, 2010.

- Coelho, Paulo. THE ALCHEMIST. HarperOne, 1993.

- Grandin, Temple. THINKING IN PICTURES. Vintage, 2006.

Chapter 20: Sacred Structure and Routines

- Dunn, Winnie. LIVING SENSATIONALLY: UNDERSTANDING YOUR SENSES. Jessica Kingsley Publishers, 2008.

- Koenig, Kathleen, & Rudney, Susan. SENSORY PROCESSING AND SELF-REGULATION. AOTA Press, 2010.

- Siegel, Daniel J., & Bryson, Tina Payne. THE POWER OF SHOWING UP. Ballantine Books, 2020.
- Grandin, Temple. THE WAY I SEE IT. Future Horizons, 2020.
- Myles, Brenda Smith. ASPERGER SYNDROME AND DIFFICULT MOMENTS. AAPC Publishing, 2014.
- Greenspan, Stanley. THE CHALLENGING CHILD. Da Capo Lifelong Books, 2007.
- Al-Ghani, K. I. THE RED BEAST: CONTROLLING ANGER IN CHILDREN WITH ASPERGER'S SYNDROME. Jessica Kingsley Publishers, 2008.

Chapter 21: Mindfulness and Grounding Practices

- Kabat-Zinn, Jon. FULL CATASTROPHE LIVING. Bantam, 2013.
- Bogdashina, Olga. SENSORY PERCEPTUAL ISSUES IN AUTISM AND ASPERGER SYNDROME. Jessica Kingsley, 2016.
- Siegel, Daniel J. THE MINDFUL BRAIN. W.W. Norton, 2007.
- Williams, Donna. SOMEBODY SOMEWHERE: BREAKING FREE FROM THE WORLD OF AUTISM. Times Books, 1994.
- Brach, Tara. RADICAL ACCEPTANCE. Bantam, 2003.
- Wallace, B. Alan. THE ATTENTION REVOLUTION. Wisdom Publications, 2006.
- Greenland, Susan Kaiser. THE MINDFUL CHILD. Free Press, 2010.

Chapter 22: Developing Sacred Rapport

- Rogers, Carl R. ON BECOMING A PERSON. Houghton Mifflin, 1961.
- Siegel, Daniel J. THE POWER OF SHOWING UP. Ballantine, 2020.
- Greene, Ross. THE EXPLOSIVE CHILD. Harper, 2014.
- Greenspan, Stanley I. THE GROWTH OF THE MIND. Perseus Books, 1999.
- Attwood, Tony. THE COMPLETE GUIDE TO ASPERGER'S SYNDROME. Jessica Kingsley, 2006.
- Neufeld, Gordon & Maté, Gabor. HOLD ON TO YOUR KIDS. Ballantine Books, 2006.

- Sainsbury, Clare. MARTIAN IN THE PLAYGROUND. Sage Publications, 2009.

Chapter 23: Ethical Empowerment

- Bascom, Julia. LOUD HANDS: AUTISTIC PEOPLE, SPEAKING. Autistic Self Advocacy Network, 2012.

- Kapp, Steven. AUTISM AND THE SOCIAL MODEL. Palgrave Macmillan, 2019.

- Neumeier, Sebastian. AUTISTIC COMMUNITY AND THE NEURODIVERSITY MOVEMENT. Springer, 2020.

- Brown, Brené. DARING GREATLY: HOW THE COURAGE TO BE VULNERABLE TRANSFORMS THE WAY WE LIVE, LOVE, PARENT, AND LEAD. Avery, 2012.

- Milton, Damian. THE NEURODIVERSITY READER. Pavilion Publishing, 2020.

- Prizant, Barry. UNIQUELY HUMAN: A DIFFERENT WAY OF SEEING AUTISM. Simon & Schuster, 2015.

- Manrique, Sarah. EMPOWERED AUTISM. Rooted Spirit Press, 2021.

Chapter 24: Caring for the Whole Being

- Prizant, Barry. UNIQUELY HUMAN: A DIFFERENT WAY OF SEEING AUTISM. Simon & Schuster, 2015.

- Siegel, Daniel J. & Bryson, Tina Payne. THE WHOLE-BRAIN CHILD. Delacorte Press, 2011.

- Hart, Tobin. THE SECRET SPIRITUAL WORLD OF CHILDREN. New World Library, 2003.

- Neff, Kristin. SELF-COMPASSION: THE PROVEN POWER OF BEING KIND TO YOURSELF. William Morrow, 2011.

- Greenspan, Stanley. THE GROWTH OF THE MIND AND THE ENDANGERED ORIGINS OF INTELLIGENCE. Perseus Books, 1997.

- Woodbine, Rachel. HOLISTIC AUTISM SUPPORT. Inner Well Press, 2020.

- Cozolino, Louis. THE NEUROSCIENCE OF HUMAN RELATIONSHIPS. Norton, 2014.

SECTION THREE: For Autism Advocates

Chapter 25: The Spiritual Power of Neurodiversity

- Silberman, Steve. NEUROTRIBES: THE LEGACY OF AUTISM AND THE FUTURE OF NEURODIVERSITY. Avery, 2015.

- Kapp, Steven. AUTISTIC COMMUNITY AND THE NEURODIVERSITY MOVEMENT. Springer, 2020.

- Bascom, Julia. LOUD HANDS: AUTISTIC PEOPLE, SPEAKING. Autistic Self Advocacy Network, 2012.

- Milton, Damian. THE NEURODIVERSITY READER. Pavilion Publishing, 2020.

- Manrique, Sarah. EMPOWERED AUTISM. Rooted Spirit Press, 2021.

- Singer, Judy. NEURODIVERSITY: THE BIRTH OF AN IDEA. Amazon Digital, 2016.

- Sacks, Oliver. AN ANTHROPOLOGIST ON MARS. Knopf, 1995.

Chapter 26: Centering Autistic Voices

- Bascom, Julia. LOUD HANDS: AUTISTIC PEOPLE, SPEAKING. Autistic Self Advocacy Network, 2012.

- Biklen, Douglas. AUTISM AND THE MYTH OF THE PERSON ALONE. NYU Press, 2005.

- Baggs, Amanda. WHAT EVERY AUTISTIC PERSON WISHES YOU KNEW. Self-Published, 2008.

- Sequenzia, Ibby Grace. THE ABCS OF AUTISM ACCEPTANCE. Autonomous Press, 2016.

- Endow, Judy. LEARNING THE HIDDEN CURRICULUM. AAPC Publishing, 2012.

- Russo, Melanie. I AM AUTISTIC AND I HAVE A VOICE. Unity Press, 2021.

- Ortega, Remy. SPEAKING ON THE SPECTRUM. Open Field Books, 2019.

Chapter 27: Dignity for All

- Kim, Eunjung. CURATING ACCESS: DISABILITY ART ACTIVISM AND THE POLITICS OF DIGNITY. Duke University Press, 2016.

- Brown, Brené. DARING GREATLY. Avery, 2012.
- Clare, Eli. BRILLIANT IMPERFECTION: GRAPPLING WITH CURE. Duke University Press, 2017.
- Mingus, Mia. LEAVING EVIDENCE: ESSAYS ON DISABILITY JUSTICE. Self-Published, 2021.
- Lorde, Audre. SISTER OUTSIDER. Crossing Press, 1984.
- Berne, Patty. DISABILITY JUSTICE: A WORKING DRAFT. Sins Invalid, 2015.
- Neumeier, Sebastian. AUTISTIC COMMUNITY AND THE NEURODIVERSITY MOVEMENT. Springer, 2020.

Chapter 28: Creating Sacred Inclusion

- Ault, Monica. INCLUSIVE SPIRITUALITY: EMBRACING NEURODIVERSE WORSHIP. Harmony Press, 2010.
- Brown, Thomas. WELCOMING ALL: NEURODIVERSITY IN FAITH COMMUNITIES. Sacred Path Press, 2016.
- Mount, Kristina. NEURODIVERGENT AND HOLY: STORIES FROM THE MARGINS. Unity Books, 2022.
- Yergeau, Melanie. AUTHORING AUTISM: ON RHETORIC AND NEUROLOGICAL QUEERNESS. Duke University Press, 2017.
- Bass, Diana Butler. CHRISTIANITY AFTER RELIGION. HarperOne, 2012.
- Koenig, Harold. SPIRITUALITY AND HEALTH RESEARCH. Templeton Press, 2012.
- Broderick, Alicia. DISABILITY STUDIES AND THE INCLUSIVE SPIRIT. Nova Publishing, 2019.

Chapter 29: Educating with Love and Light

- Palmer, Parker J. THE COURAGE TO TEACH. Jossey-Bass, 1998.
- hooks, bell. TEACHING TO TRANSGRESS: EDUCATION AS THE PRACTICE OF FREEDOM. Routledge, 1994.
- Ginsburg, Kenneth R. BUILDING RESILIENCE IN CHILDREN AND TEENS. AAP Publishing, 2020.

- Montessori, Maria. THE SECRET OF CHILDHOOD. Ballantine Books, 1966.
- Ault, Monica. INCLUSIVE SPIRITUALITY: EMBRACING NEURODIVERSE WORSHIP. Harmony Press, 2010.
- Neufeld, Gordon. HOLD ON TO YOUR KIDS. Ballantine Books, 2006.
- Kame'enui, Edward. EFFECTIVE TEACHING STRATEGIES THAT ACCOMMODATE DIVERSE LEARNERS. Pearson, 2012.

Chapter 30: Language That Honors the Soul

- Biklen, Douglas. AUTISM AND THE MYTH OF THE PERSON ALONE. NYU Press, 2005.
- Sinclair, Jim. DON'T MOURN FOR US. Autistic Self Advocacy Network, 1993.
- Baggs, Mel. WHAT EVERY AUTISTIC PERSON WISHES YOU KNEW. Self-published, 2008.
- Yergeau, Melanie. AUTHORING AUTISM: ON RHETORIC AND NEUROLOGICAL QUEERNESS. Duke University Press, 2017.
- Neumeier, Sebastian. AUTISTIC COMMUNITY AND THE NEURODIVERSITY MOVEMENT. Springer, 2020.
- Robison, John Elder. LOOK ME IN THE EYE. Crown Publishing, 2007.
- Bascom, Julia. LOUD HANDS: AUTISTIC PEOPLE, SPEAKING. Autistic Self Advocacy Network, 2012.

Chapter 31: Justice as Spiritual Imperative

- Hooks, Bell. ALL ABOUT LOVE: NEW VISIONS. William Morrow, 2000.
- West, Cornel. RACE MATTERS. Beacon Press, 1993.
- Freire, Paulo. PEDAGOGY OF THE OPPRESSED. Continuum, 1970.
- Crenshaw, Kimberlé. ON INTERSECTIONALITY. New Press, 2017.
- Lorde, Audre. SISTER OUTSIDER. Crossing Press, 1984.
- Brown, Brené. DARE TO LEAD. Random House, 2018.
- Minahan, Jessica & Rappaport, Nancy. THE BEHAVIOR CODE. Harvard Education Press, 2012.

Chapter 32: Infusing Policy with Purpose

- Taylor, Steven J. AUTISM AND THE ETHICS OF INCLUSION. DSQ, 2010.

- Kapp, Steven. AUTISM AND THE SOCIAL MODEL. Palgrave Macmillan, 2019.

- Crenshaw, Kimberlé. ON INTERSECTIONALITY. New Press, 2017.

- Nussbaum, Martha. FRONTIERS OF JUSTICE. Harvard University Press, 2006.

- Roberts, Dorothy E. KILLING THE BLACK BODY. Vintage, 1997.

- Davis, Lennard J. THE DISABILITY STUDIES READER. Routledge, 2016.

- Lawson, Wendy. BUILD YOUR OWN LIFE: A SELF-HELP GUIDE FOR INDIVIDUALS WITH ASPERGER'S SYNDROME. Jessica Kingsley, 2001.

Chapter 33: Empowering the Spirit of the Advocate

- Lorde, Audre. SISTER OUTSIDER: ESSAYS AND SPEECHES. Crossing Press, 1984.

- West, Cornel. DEMOCRACY MATTERS. Penguin Books, 2004.

- Ritchie, Amanda. NEURODIVERGENT ADVOCACY FROM THE INSIDE OUT. Voices Press, 2021.

- McIntosh, Peggy. WHITE PRIVILEGE: UNPACKING THE INVISIBLE KNAPSACK. Wellesley College, 1988.

- Brown, Brené. RISING STRONG. Spiegel & Grau, 2015.

- Kearney, Richard. ANATHEISM: RETURNING TO GOD AFTER GOD. Columbia University Press, 2009.

- Bascom, Julia. LOUD HANDS: AUTISTIC PEOPLE, SPEAKING. Autistic Self Advocacy Network, 2012.

Chapter 34: Redefining Safety with Compassion

- Prizant, Barry M. UNIQUELY HUMAN. Simon & Schuster, 2015.

- Van Der Kolk, Bessel. THE BODY KEEPS THE SCORE. Penguin, 2014.

- Maté, Gabor. SCATTERED MINDS. Knopf Canada, 1999.
- Siegel, Daniel J. THE WHOLE-BRAIN CHILD. Bantam, 2011.
- Greene, Ross W. THE EXPLOSIVE CHILD. Harper, 2014.
- Gray, Carol. THE NEW SOCIAL STORY BOOK. Future Horizons, 2010.
- Delahooke, Mona. BEYOND BEHAVIORS. PESI Publishing, 2019.

Chapter 35: Building Conscious Communities

- Wheatley, Margaret J. TURNING TO ONE ANOTHER. Berrett-Koehler, 2002.
- Palmer, Parker J. A HIDDEN WHOLENESS. Jossey-Bass, 2004.
- hooks, bell. BELONGING: A CULTURE OF PLACE. Routledge, 2008.
- Lorde, Audre. SISTER OUTSIDER. Crossing Press, 1984.
- DiAngelo, Robin. WHAT DOES IT MEAN TO BE WHITE? Peter Lang, 2012.
- Kretzmann, John P., and McKnight, John L. BUILDING COMMUNITIES FROM THE INSIDE OUT. ACTA Publications, 1993.
- O'Hara, Maureen. THE PRACTICE OF PARTICIPATORY SPIRITUALITY. New World Library, 2010.

Chapter 36: Affirming Sacred Purpose

- Palmer, Parker J. LET YOUR LIFE SPEAK. Jossey-Bass, 2000.
- Vanier, Jean. BECOMING HUMAN. Paulist Press, 1998.
- Merton, Thomas. NO MAN IS AN ISLAND. Houghton Mifflin Harcourt, 1955.
- Coelho, Paulo. THE ALCHEMIST. HarperOne, 1993.
- Rohr, Richard. FALLING UPWARD. Jossey-Bass, 2011.
- Nouwen, Henri. LIFE OF THE BELOVED. Crossroad Publishing, 1992.
- Kaur, Valarie. SEE NO STRANGER. One World, 2020.

NOTES:

NOTES:

NOTES:

www.ingramcontent.com/pod-product-compliance
Lightning Source LLC
Chambersburg PA
CBHW070047080526
44586CB00013B/953